Could Jesus Walk on Water?

164 Questions and Answers about the Faith

Monika Deitenbeck,
Marcus C. Leitschuh,
Christina Riecke, and
Brother Paul Terwitte

HiddenSpring

D0916473

Cover design by Trudi Gershenov
Book design by Lynn Else

Copyright © 2005 by Bonifatius Verlag/Joh. Brendow & Sohn Verlag, Germany

This edition is published by arrangement with Claudia Böhme Rights and Literary Agency, Hannover, Germany (www.agency-boehme.com). Originally published as *Konnte Jesus übers Wasser gehen?*

English translation copyright © 2007 by Paulist Press, Inc.

Library of Congress Cataloging-in-Publication Data

Konnte Jesus übers Wasser gehen? English.
    Could Jesus walk on water? : 164 questions and answers about the faith / Monika Deitenbeck...[et al.].
    p. cm.
    ISBN 978-1-58768-040-3 (pbk. : alk. paper)
    1. Christianity—Miscellanea. 2. Christian life—Miscellanea.
I. Deitenbeck, Monika. II. Title.
    BR121.3.K6613 2007
    230—dc22

2006034289

HiddenSpring
An imprint of Paulist Press
997 Macarthur Boulevard
Mahwah, New Jersey 07430

www.hiddenspringbooks.com

Printed and bound in the
United States of America

Contents

INTRODUCTION:
In the Beginning—
My Questions about Faith

Questions arise at the beginning of faith. Perhaps that is why the Bible gives us so many questions:

When she was nearly one hundred years old, Sarah could still give birth. Jesus walks on water. After his resurrection, the disciples caught exactly 153 fish (John 21:11) from the Sea of Tiberias.

The puzzles of the Bible are put together for enlightened people because they know that there is more to learn than simply biology or chemistry.

To find the message behind things we have to keep on asking questions. There is a statement in the Bible: "When a child asks you questions" (Deut 6:20). Connected with this statement is the challenge directed at adults to explain their faith and make it understandable to children.

A year ago such questions were directed to us on our website. We, Evangelical and Catholic Christians with very different occupations and activities, have one thing in common. As Christians we believe in God and want to tell others about his love and want to answer the questions as best we can. Of course we do not know everything and maybe one or another of you could even formulate a better answer.

All the answers in this book are very personal. Religion teachers, pastors, or friends in your neighborhood would probably answer them differently. Even that could become exciting for you: to compare, to think for yourself, and then find questions of your own. It would be great for us if our thoughts would give you the courage to find your own answers and then hand them on to us.

We wish you much joy in reading—and we hope that you will experience the joy of the apostles when they caught their fish. Find out that God can do more than we dare to believe.

Monika Deitenbeck
Marcus C. Leitschuh
Christina Riecke
Brother Paul Terwitte

ONE
EVERYDAY CONCERNS

Acceptance, Foreigners, Parents, Happiness,
Marriage, Children, Contraception, Sickness, Life,
Sadness, Love, Fate, Homosexuality, Sex, Fun,
Death, Forgiveness, Chance, the Future

The Future

YOUR QUESTION: What does the future hold for me?

SENDER: John, 14

RESPONDER: Christina Riecke

May I ask you a question in return? What are you bringing to your own future? What do you want to do with your life? What will your contribution look like? For what do you want to be famous or known? What do you want others to say about you?

Maybe your response is: "John earns a good salary" or "John is always there for others" or "John is there only for himself" or "John has an idea that gives hope to many people in the future." What the future will bring for you depends greatly on yourself. I wish you God's blessing for your future. And may you be a blessing for many others.

SUBMIT

Fear of Death

How do I overcome the fear of death?

SENDER: Stan, 18

RESPONDER: Brother Paul Terwitte

To pray as Jesus did can help: "Father, into your hands I place my life." I say that prayer with many other Christians each evening. To me falling asleep is like a little letting go and dying. This prayer builds my confidence in God. It enlarges me when I begin to fear that I must give up things, or when I become disappointed, or because I don't know what is coming next. Those are all little deaths. Every day I place my life in God's hands—and at the end, I'll place it in God's hands forever.

SUBMIT

To Honor Parents?

YOUR QUESTION: It is written in the Bible: "Honor your father and your mother." Right after I was born, my father left my mother. Because of that, my mother drinks. When she is drunk she is impossible. If she has not been drinking, she is irritable because she needs to drink. How am I supposed to honor the two and why?

SENDER: Johanna, 15

RESPONDER: Marcus C. Leitschuh

You were called into life by God. That your father and your mother are such irresponsible parents is a terrible thing for you. But it is a fact: Even through these people, God can create a person who can think earnestly and choose to become better than her parents. "To honor parents" means to see them with the eyes of God. To honor them also means to face them concerning their wrongdoing, to correct them about it, to be forgiving, and to find ways to truly help them.

In the letter to the Colossians it is written that women should love their husbands and husbands should treat their wives well, and also that children should honor their parents. And further on it says: "Fathers, do not provoke your children, or they may lose heart" (Col 3:21). God did not tell us to love injustice, addiction to drugs, or abuse. One can honor parents best by speaking to them truthfully and lovingly.

SUBMIT

| YOUR QUESTION: | Does God love even those who have AIDS? |

| SENDER: | Thomas, 14 |

| RESPONDER: | Christina Riecke |

God definitely loves people with AIDS. God loves all people without exception, no matter what they have done or what was done to them.

And a little more concretely, Jesus once said: If you visit a sick person, it is like visiting me (see Matt 25:36). I have personally experienced how people with AIDS in Germany, Africa, and India were considered outcasts from their families. That is not what God wishes. Luckily, I have also experienced how other people care for those with AIDS, how they protect them, how they fight for their rights and for their right to be heard, how they are with them. Jesus says: "Whoever does that, meets me."

SUBMIT

The Separated

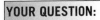

YOUR QUESTION: May separated Christians marry again?

SENDER: Andrew, 15

RESPONDER: Brother Paul Terwitte

In the Catholic Church the answer to that question is a clear no, unless the first marriage was not a valid one. Marrying means that man and woman, husband and wife, give themselves freely to each other for the rest of their lives. That is much more than just staying with a person until someone better comes along. Married people must do everything to renew this union faithfully throughout their lives. If they separate they cannot simply take back their promise to God. The connection that the government calls "marriage", is, in God's eyes, a connection that even after a painful failure may still become a blessing.

YOUR QUESTION: My question is really a touchy matter. It concerns homosexuals. Are they loved by God? I have friends who think so. I never thought they were wrong. Now I am being told they are wrong. I am waiting for your answer.

SENDER: Julia, 18

RESPONDER: Brother Paul Terwitte

Homosexuals, who make up at least 5% of humankind, are loved by God as much as heterosexuals. For both groups what matters are the acts they perform as a consequence of this love.

All people are called by God to live chaste lives. An overall condemnation of homosexuals is wrong. This would not be in accord with the will of God, who knows and loves every single person.

SUBMIT

Someone Who
Spoils My Fun

I like to have fun. But the church has all these laws that keep people from having fun. Doesn't the church understand that people need to have some fun?

Tom, 15

Marcus C. Leitschuh

No one in the church has anything against "fun." There was a time people questioned whether Jesus laughed. I am certain he understood fun. Some of his stories are very original and make us smile. Jesus must have not only fished in Lake Genesaret, but he surely also bathed there and probably splashed water on his friends. But Jesus and the church ask us repeatedly if we are having "fun" only for the sake of fun. To be human also means to be responsible. The great seriousness with which the church celebrates the joy about God in liturgical services arises from the respect the church has for God. And since we have entrusted ourselves completely to God, serious consequences follow, but also a certain freedom. Joking around is fun for a while, but real joy continues to the end. Religious services do not always sound like fun, but the "Alleluia" is nothing other than laughing joyfully against death and all the tragedies of the world—because Jesus helped people unerringly to a new life, because he went directly from death to life in the resurrection to give us true joy.

YOUR QUESTION: Is it still worthwhile to bring children into the world?

SENDER: Sandra, 19

RESPONDER: Christina Riecke

I completely understand your question, since I often asked myself the same thing: "Do I have enough hope to have a child?" But my perspective changed, especially after I experienced the birth of my own child: "A child who gives me great hope." When a child looks at me, smiles, and asks me something, or shows me one of her discoveries or a game, I think: "God is looking at me directly, touching me, greeting me."

Is this world still worth its existence? Each day I am fascinated by the fact that God has not given up yet—that, full of hope, he lets the sun rise and he loves each of his children.

SUBMIT

Accepting Myself

YOUR QUESTION: How can I learn to accept my appearance (what I don't like about the way I look)?

SENDER: Alina, 19

RESPONDER: Brother Paul Terwitte

Say to yourself, "I am unique." God created you as an original. There won't be someone like you again. Don't waste your time trying to copy someone else. God wants to reveal himself to others through you and perhaps exactly through what you don't like about yourself. Develop your abilities. Show yourself to others as you really are. If they do not want to accept you as you are, the way God made you, forgive them. Eventually they too will learn that people who value their own uniqueness are happier than people who just copy everybody else.

SUBMIT

A Good Christian

What must I do to be a good Christian?

SENDER: Jacob, 17

RESPONDER: Brother Paul Terwitte

Walk with Jesus as with a big brother; whoever does this is a good Christian—so long as you understand what "walking with Jesus" means. Whoever understands that one belongs to Jesus irrevocably through baptism shows the consequences of "belonging to Jesus." For example, you belong to a community of the sisters and brothers of Jesus. Meet with them regularly. You, like Jesus, have a love for the poor. Decide to help them regularly. You know, just as Jesus did, what is really important in life. Spend ten minutes each morning and evening reading the Bible and praying and, in this way, take time for God.

SUBMIT

Sex before Marriage

YOUR QUESTION: The church teaches that sex before marriage is forbidden. What makes sex different when you are married?

SENDER: Mike, 13

RESPONDER: Marcus C. Leitschuh

The church believes that each level of a relationship between lovers has a type of sexual attraction. To discover this treasure is one of the most beautiful challenges of male and female friends. The church cares about the fact that the beauty of love should be truly enjoyed to the full. If you look in old churches you will see how erotic some of the paintings are. The best and deepest sign a man and wife can give to each other is sexual love. For Jesus, marriage is a trusting relationship because the people involved have promised themselves to each other before God. Only then can two people give themselves totally to each other without worrying that one of them might leave to "find something better." Within a faithful marriage, people can give themselves so completely to each other that their sexual love becomes a truly powerful experience.

SUBMIT

13

Content with Life

How much can faith be an essential part of life?

SENDER: Mark, 18

RESPONDER: Brother Paul Terwitte

Faith is living love. I myself cannot imagine a life without faith in God. God created me. He wanted me to be what I am and not different. He is there to speak to me every day and challenges me daily with ideas to build a world. Without God I would be like a fish without water and a flower without sunshine. I would not be able to live. For me, not an hour passes that I do not thank, complain, or sing—to the God of my life.

Church Marriage

YOUR QUESTION: Why should people be married in the church?

SENDER: Rebecca, 25

RESPONDER: Christina Riecke

I myself am a married woman. Our church wedding was very meaningful for me. Allowing my marriage to be blessed by God affected me on a really deep level. I believe that marriage is God's idea and that he protects it.

One may think that the church's blessing makes the marriage holy, that it creates a holy thing out of a worldly one, and that it makes a divine action out of the world of tables and benches and the courtroom.

The Bible says exactly the opposite—that life is holy. It is untouchable because it belongs to God. Each person is precious. Through God's blessings all the goods of the earth become "enjoyable." For example, prayer before meals does not make the bread holy but the holy bread that God lets grow from the earth is given to us to enjoy through prayer. Creation is protected by God. If we take something without thanking God for it or asking for his blessing we simply grab it and forget its origin.

At my wedding celebration in church I said to my husband and my husband said to me: "For me you are holy and you are a gift of God to me."

SUBMIT

YOUR QUESTION: Does God help when I have a toothache?

SENDER: Paul, 12

RESPONDER: Marcus C. Leitschuh

God's help cannot be swallowed like a painkiller. As a rule he does not help against toothaches, which have their own causes. If you don't brush your teeth, you'll get cavities. God cannot do anything about that. God helps me when I have a toothache by strengthening my common sense and giving me the courage to follow the right path: to the dentist.

The Bible often speaks of miraculous healings, but that does not happen very often today. Still in times of crisis there are signs of hope. Maybe you'll see small signs from God. Jesus often says after performing a miracle, "Your faith has made you whole." A faith that supports us in hopeless situations and always gives us refuge in God can indeed be very healing.

SUBMIT

The Meaning of Life

What is the meaning of life?

SENDER: Leslie, 14

RESPONDER: Brother Paul Terwitte

To love God. To love yourself. To love your neighbor.

To love God: See yourself as God's creature. Thank him for being with you. Tell him your sufferings.

To love yourself: No matter what others may say, the most important thing is to remember that God created you. Because he loves you, feel important and fully develop yourself to God's great joy.

To love your neighbor: Even though there are some very unpleasant people in the world, see them all as God's children. You do not have to embrace each one. But you must be good to each one, even though that person may not be nice to you—that you can do.

SUBMIT

To Forgive Again and Again?

My girlfriend is always mad at me. Do I really have to forgive her?

SENDER: Susanne, 13

RESPONDER: Christina Riecke

At the time when Jesus lived, there was a Roman law that said, "A Roman can force a Jew to walk a mile with him and carry his baggage." The people asked Jesus, "Do we always have to do that?" Jesus had an idea. He did not say, "No, you do not have to do that because that is completely humiliating." Nor did he say, "Yes, you have to do it. Endure the humiliation quietly." He said something entirely new, something very different. "When someone forces you to go a mile with him, do it. And then go a second mile with him." Why is that? What happens on the second mile? The Roman notices that he is not forcing you, he has no power over you—you go with him of your own free will, farther than you have to go. The Roman asks himself why you would do this for him and begins to talk to you. At the end of the journey you might not have become best friends, but you have shared your road and maybe even a glass of water....

SUBMIT

Love and
Falling in Love

YOUR QUESTION: Is it possible to fall in love with a certain person more than once in your life?

SENDER: Caroline, 14

RESPONDER: Brother Paul Terwitte

Emotions can be powerful. We meet so many people that it is inevitable we will fall in love at some point in our lives. At such moments, be careful not to stop thinking. It may hurt, but say no if you have to. You are more than an emotion. Falling in love has to be a free decision to really love another person. True love remains faithful to the person we love and does not allow itself to be distracted, even if we develop intense feelings for someone else. You can often fall in love with other people or things, but true love must be very special.

SUBMIT

YOUR QUESTION: Why oh why is this happening to me now?

SENDER: Josh, 19

RESPONDER: Monika Deitenbeck

I really don't know what is happening in your life at this moment, but I do know one thing: life is exciting, many-faceted, and full of surprises. We are always in the middle of life and help to shape it.
Life is not simply full of trouble in one way or another. Life is always what we make of it or what it will do for us. It is very good and helpful if we ask God's advice and care to be a part of our life.

SUBMIT

Only One Faith?

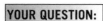

YOUR QUESTION: Do I have to stay in my religion?

SENDER: Leslie, 14

RESPONDER: Brother Paul Terwitte

Whatever happens, you will remain with God because he remains with you. How you get to know him better will become the most fascinating story of your life. It can actually happen that a Catholic decides to become an Evangelical—or the other way around. People of the Jewish faith may realize, as Edith Stein did: "I find something of God in Jesus, something that I have been searching for all my life." But even there, the opposite can happen. So it could be that you will not stay with your faith. The important thing, however, is that you remain always with God.

SUBMIT

YOUR QUESTION: Why does God give us life?

SENDER: Maren, 19

RESPONDER: Monika Deitenbeck

Because God does not want to live alone. He is a creative God who has planned something very special for each and every one of us because he loves us. God wants us to be as creative as he is and develop ourselves and all our capabilities so that we can perfect our world. God wants us to live joyfully, to talk to him, to thank him, to treasure him and to foster a deep relationship with him.

SUBMIT

Faith

YOUR QUESTION: Does it make any difference what one believes? The essential thing is to believe.

SENDER: Carsten, 14

RESPONDER: Brother Paul Terwitte

To believe is one thing. *What* one believes must be the right thing. Human beings want to know the truth, but because they are not God, they must do so in their time and with what means they have. Whoever is honest in the search will respect everyone who is as serious about that search as the seeker is. Christians go one step further. They believe and acknowledge that God meets humans halfway. Whoever believes in Jesus accepts God's help in the search for the true faith.

SUBMIT

YOUR QUESTION: I am being asked again and again why the pope is so against contraceptives, even though there is no protection against AIDS in the third world and many people die of AIDS.

SENDER: Chris, 24

RESPONDER: Brother Paul Terwitte

The pope is against contraceptives as a general solution for the difficulties that people have in regulating their sexual activities. Of course the pope knows that many people remain safe and healthy even though they have sexual relations with more than one person. But the pope also knows that this kind of relating is against the teaching of Jesus. Jesus showed human beings that they could not become happy when they satisfy only their lust. Sex is great, but it must be reserved for stable relationships. Therefore it is better to support people in keeping their sexuality in check. The best support for that is a good Christian education, oriented toward Christian principles. Therefore the pope and many Christians support good schools rather than the distribution of free contraceptives.

SUBMIT

Aliens

SENDER: Tim, 14

RESPONDER: Monika Deitenbeck

I have no idea! Some people feel that there are aliens "out there." That is not really an issue for me. If there is life beyond earth, then that life would also be loved by God. In any case, we are on the planet visited by God when he became human. That distinguishes us from others. God has loved us, lived here, and paid for us with his life and so saved the world from being lost in certain death.

SUBMIT

25

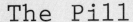

The Pill

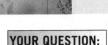

YOUR QUESTION: Did God forbid the pill?

SENDER: Corinna, 14

RESPONDER: Brother Paul Terwitte

Love is the creation of God. According to his intention, love should be lived. I am sorry to say that everyone understands love in a different way. The Catholic Church wants to protect love in the name of Jesus. The church says about the pill: besides the promise of faithful love, justice is also needed. The pill chemically interferes with a woman's biological functions in order to prevent the creation of human life. Two people have to be responsible in their vocation as parents by sharing happiness and burdens together and watch for your fertile and infertile days.

SUBMIT

Unhappiness

Why am I unhappy?

SENDER: Matt, 23

RESPONDER: Monika Deitenbeck

Unhappiness can have many reasons. One thing is necessary: look at it honestly. How do I view my life? Do I ask what is good and what is not good? Do I need to change some things that I am doing? Do I go at it with God's help? What are my crosses? Can I place them in God's hands with the petition to make my shoulders strong enough to carry them? Discover the answers to these questions: Where did I come from? Where am I going and why? I am loved, wanted, treasured, and important, and I can help to build my future now. Everything will be rewarded, even what goes wrong.

SUBMIT

Why Does God Let This Happen?

YOUR QUESTION: Why must my dear grandmother suffer even though she truly believes in God?

SENDER: Mark, 25

RESPONDER: Brother Paul Terwitte

Such questions are worth consideration, but there is really no answer. Neither is there a reason for a healthy and happy life (yet no one honestly asks, "Why am I healthy?"). Good and bad experiences can open a person's mind to God. Even if your grandmother must suffer a lot, the same things happen to many other people. If she has faith, she will say with the dying Jesus on the cross, "Father in heaven, into your hands I place my life."

SUBMIT

Meaning of Life

YOUR QUESTION: What is the meaning of life?

SENDER: Steve, 18

RESPONDER: Monika Deitenbeck

With our gifts and limitations, our possibilities and abilities, whatever makes us who and what we are, we live for the glory of God. We exist and develop our abilities so that we can make it easier for others to live, to love, to suffer, and to believe.

SUBMIT

YOUR QUESTION: What will my future be like?

SENDER: Brian, 17

RESPONDER: Monika Deitenbeck

It may not be easy to live in the future or in the future world, but we are never alone. Jesus, the Lord of the World, the Risen Lord, is always present. Because he lives, everything will be rewarded; nothing will be lost. There will always be strength and purpose, and our trust in him will always be fulfilled. He is everything for us and will not leave us alone. Each one of us is as important as if there were no one except us.

SUBMIT

Why Am I This Way?

Why am I the way I am and not different?

Linda, 16

Christina Riecke

There is an old legend. (Legends are stories that are not true but want to point out some truth.) The angels in heaven saw how, again and again, God went behind a curtain in his apartment each time that he created a new human being. The angels knew that creating a new human being was one of God's favorite activities. He had never made any duplicates.

Once an inquisitive angel peeked behind the curtain and discovered that God looked into a mirror each time he was creating a human being.

You are an original. In your own special way you reflect one of God's unique characteristics.

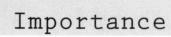

YOUR QUESTION: Am I important?

SENDER: Jessica, 15

RESPONDER: Monika Deitenbeck

Of course you are! Your abilities are yours alone. What you think, how you laugh, see the sky, accept your life—only you do it in this particular way. No one else can do what you are doing. You, like everyone else, are one of God's original creations, one of his favorite ideas. Only you can live your designated way and fill your designated place in life. No one else! Only you!

SUBMIT

Just As I Am

YOUR QUESTION: Am I acceptable to others just as I am?

SENDER: Daniela, 14

RESPONDER: Monika Deitenbeck

We all have that wish and would like to have it fulfilled during our entire life. Sometimes we learn very slowly to accept ourselves. When I say yes to the way I am, I should be happy about my strengths—but I should not overlook my weaknesses. Often understanding that is the key to acceptance. If I can accept my weaknesses, then others will also. If God can tolerate us, accept us, and work with what we are and have, we should also tolerate ourselves, and the other people can follow.

SUBMIT

A Good Christian

YOUR QUESTION: What do I have to do to be a good Christian?

SENDER: Jacob, 17

RESPONDER: Christina Riecke

I don't exactly know what a "good Christian" is. Jesus once provokingly said, "No one is good but God alone" (Luke 18:19). I can imagine myself saying: "This person is a convincing Christian!" or "She is an authentic Christian," which means that she does what she says, or lives what she preaches. Such persons try hard to make sure their actions are consistent with their words. In my opinion, the most beautiful statement one can make about Christians would be, "They reflect in their lives the fact that Jesus is their light. They shine because 'the Light' shines on them."

SUBMIT

Chance

Should I give my life over to chance?

SENDER: Lina, 16

RESPONDER: Monika Deitenbeck

No, definitely not. Give it over to the risen Christ. He who made you knows what he wants you to be. His greatest interest lies in the hope that our lives will not disappear in the sand but that they will be successful. People who count on Jesus will usually end up well. Don't play with chance. Keep your eyes open to see where you can enter an open door. Imagine that it has been opened for you. Trusting and going forward belong together.

SUBMIT

Only During Troubled Times?

Many people in our neighborhood live well. Why should we convince them that they have a problem and need God? Isn't it possible that their lives could continue along this good path? And why do people suddenly think about God when they run into problems?

SENDER: Sarah, 14

RESPONDER: Christina Riecke

Last year I bought a fast new car. After I rode about one hundred miles, I arrived at my friend's home. In the parking lot I had a little accident involving a parking sign. I was very upset—my new car already had a dent!
I took the car to a mechanic and when he was finished, we couldn't get the car started! My mechanic then discovered that the gasoline pump was not working. With any other car I would not have been surprised that something was broken—but not with this one! The mechanic told me: "You were very lucky to discover this problem when you did. It could have been very dangerous." Then I was really happy about my little accident.

I think that is how many people live—as if their lives were like a new car. From the outside everything looks great. They drive full force throughout their lives without knowing that their lives are in danger. Maybe one small accident makes them stop and think and check things out....Others continue to race.

SUBMIT

Why Pray?

YOUR QUESTION: What do we get out of praying?

SENDER: Tom, 15

RESPONDER: Christina Riecke

"What does it do for us?" This is a very essential question. You invest money and make a profit. You study and get a good grade. You pay and you receive a product that you choose. You take time for someone and he helps you. Relationships are mutually helpful. "We pat each other's backs." But it is hard to say what prayer "brings" us. It has no end product. Prayer does not function like a soda machine. It is part of a story, a discussion. The question "What purpose does prayer have?" limits the meaning of prayer. It is like a performance, a song, something beautiful and poetic—actually without a specific purpose—but full of meaning. It is an expression of desire and love, of participation and engagement, and of attention. It is boundless, but we should not use prayer only to gain some kind of advantage.

SUBMIT

Does God Approve Any Love Relationship?

YOUR QUESTION: I am eighteen years old and I am in love with someone who is twenty-five. I know he is the right one. However, I am not sure if God allows such a relationship. What should I do?

SENDER: Simone, 18

RESPONDER: Monika Deitenbeck

First, what is possible can happen. One of these things that can happen is falling in love. At the age of eighteen one can really and often fall in love which is OK. God created us that way. Enjoy those feelings but know that you still have much time to dream and to be enraptured. Go at it slowly. There are many interesting characters among the opposite sex. Learn to know their fascinating characteristics and get to know different people without binding yourself to only one. Let yourself grow and mature slowly and don't "dash" into a relationship. A person who is seven years older than you can be very different. God gave you feelings, but he also gave you an intellect. Your mind tells you to go slowly. That is easier and better for the development of your personality.

SUBMIT

Love of Neighbor

YOUR QUESTION: A friend of mine told me that most people practice love of neighbor so that they will get to heaven as a reward. What do you say about that?

SENDER: Jared, 16

RESPONDER: Brother Paul Terwitte

I have also known such people. It is terrible to act for such reasons, but there are only a few who do so. They are pious and do very good deeds but only because they fear God. Such people say that everyone who believes in God and just does what he commands will go to heaven. This has little to do with Jesus. I try to help others because I am already "in heaven," in communion with Jesus. That is my motivation, which is expressed through my actions.

Besides, your friend should not judge others but should begin to practice love of neighbor without mental reservations.

SUBMIT

To Do and to Wish

The Bible says: "But strive first for the kingdom of God and his righteousness" (Matt 6:33). What should we do if we have another wish that is also important? May we have such wishes or not? And if I am looking for the kingdom of God, where and how should I search for it?

SENDER: Simone, 13

RESPONDER: Christina Riecke

The full quotation from Matthew 6:31–33 says, "Therefore do not worry, saying, 'What will we eat?' or 'What will we drink?' or 'What will we wear? For it is the Gentiles who strive for all these things; and indeed your heavenly Father knows that you need all these things. But strive first for the kingdom of God and his righteousness, and all these things will be given to you as well." Yearn for God—and God will care for you, will take care of everything you need. He will even take care of your wishes. Search! Trust your desire for God. Ask spiritual questions. Don't let yourself be distracted until you have found him. With Jesus, who talks about the kingdom of God in many different ways, you will find him who embodies the kingdom of God. If you trust in Jesus, you will find grace, eternal happiness, and your place in the kingdom of God.

TWO
WHO IS GOD?

Appearance, Giving, Believing, Talking,
Seeing, Forgiving, Forgetting, Showing,
Letting Things Happen, 9/11, Football, Harmony,
Virginity, Comas, Human Beings, Creation, Sin

Forgiving and Forgetting

YOUR QUESTION: Does God hold grudges?

SENDER: Max, 9

RESPONDER: Christina Riecke

Not at all. He forgives and forgets—and does both gladly—again and again.

SUBMIT

Where Is God?

YOUR QUESTION: Where is God?

SENDER: Dan, 16

RESPONDER: Monika Deitenbeck

God is only a prayer's distance away from us. He is like air, which we cannot see—invisible, but still there—like love, which we cannot see but can feel. We feel it and when we breathe it in, it is life-giving. God comes to us and takes care of us. He is there and does not want to be without us. He is our opportunity.

SUBMIT

Where Was God?

YOUR QUESTION: Where was God on September 11, 2001? Was he on vacation?

SENDER: Theresa, 10

RESPONDER: Marcus C. Leitschuh

Let's go even further: Was God at the controls of the two airplanes that were directed into the World Trade Center and caused the deaths of so many people? Of course not! It was people who simply wanted to terrorize and in doing so resisted the prayers directed to God. Neither Christians, Muslims, nor Jews can call on God in their terrorist actions against innocent people. At such a moment we would wish for a God who has everything under control: one who guides each person to do good as if each were a puppet, one who brings all planes to a safe landing, one who extinguishes wild forest fires, and one who rectifies every dangerous situation. But would we really want such a God, one who does not allow free will and decides everything for us, and one who decides when and whom we love? Because God gave us our free will, he lets us decide what road we want to follow; he lets us choose between good and evil. That is our difficult reality, but I would not want to have any other. On September 11, God mourned with the people who were hurt and must have tried to console the grieving.

SUBMIT

God and Jesus

YOUR QUESTION: Did God really talk to Jesus?

SENDER: Adam, 16

RESPONDER: Monika Deitenbeck

Naturally! When God became human; when he entered this world as Jesus, to redeem us from death; when he is simultaneously God in heaven and Jesus on earth, then it is clear that the two talked to each other and that Jesus used prayer to remain in contact with God. There is a beautiful song in which one line is, "Praying is talking with and listening to God." That is what Jesus did; that is what we do today. To pray is to pour out your heart before God and to listen to him, to sort out things and to let him touch us.

SUBMIT

Only What I Can See

YOUR QUESTION: What do you tell someone who says, "I believe only what I can see."

SENDER: Joseph, 11

RESPONDER: Christina Riecke

I would say, "But that is very little!" My grandmother was blind but she believed in many things that she could not see. A friend of mine, a photographer, once said, "If only I could take a photograph of God, I would have the proof of his existence." What I mean to say is that we cannot prove that God exists, but we can *experience* his existence! And it is good that we do not have a photo of God. He is mirrored in each one of us. You cannot tie God down or reduce him to a photograph. He keeps surprising you and is greater than you can imagine. Try to photograph love or generosity or oxygen. One day my friend did "experience" God. Since then he says, "Now I don't want to photograph God any more. I'd like to be his image."

SUBMIT

YOUR QUESTION: How can we imagine God? What does he look like, and more importantly, where is he?

SENDER: Katie, age unknown

RESPONDER: Monika Deitenbeck

On the first pages of the Bible it is written: "God created man and woman according to his likeness," so our mirror shows us how we should imagine God. But God also said clearly: "Do not make for yourself an image of me." He showed us who and how he is and especially what his intentions are. He came from heaven to earth as Jesus and before Jesus returned to heaven he told us, "Remember, I will always be with you."

SUBMIT

Thinking of God

YOUR QUESTION: Why do people think about God?

SENDER: Laura, 21

RESPONDER: Christina Riecke

Imagine that God had an idea about making the world and everything in it, including the sun, the oceans, the mountains, giraffes, poodles, butterflies, palm trees, raspberries, coffee beans, cinnamon, and honey. God created them and found them all beautiful. He loved the world and had every reason to be satisfied. There was only one thing missing. God wanted someone with whom he could share these beautiful things. He was longing for conversation. God did not want to be God for himself. He was even ready to share responsibility. So God created human beings out of love. Our longing for God, our search for him, our questions about him, our conscience—all are expressions of how we react to God's love. This search is part of us from our first day on earth. It is our deepest desire to live together with God in love.

SUBMIT

YOUR QUESTION: What is God?

SENDER: Dan, 16

RESPONDER: Monika Deitenbeck

The fascinating part is that God is not a "what" but a "who." The Bible talks about a God who creates humans as images of himself. He loves people as a father loves his children, one who searches for his lost son. Neither is happy without the other. They attract one another like a magnet and iron filings. With Jesus, God begins his action to bring together what belongs together so that people can discover their true homes and become strong enough to live, to die, and to live again.

SUBMIT

Imagining God

How can we imagine God?

SENDER: Lisa Marie, 16

RESPONDER: Christina Riecke

God is the creator. His son Jesus is a friend, a brother, a savior, completely human as we are and perfect as God is, the picture of the invisible God (see Col 1:15). Jesus shows us who God is and how he is: loving, merciful, and just. God loves people and wants to be near them. God is the Holy Spirit, the voice that calls you, the seeker who does not stop searching.

God as a being loves you and waits for you to come to him soon.

SUBMIT

Who Will Be Forgiven?

Whose sins does God forgive?

SENDER: Jennifer, 14

RESPONDER: Marcus C. Leitschuh

All people receive forgiveness for their sins if they honestly ask God for pardon. It does not matter if a person was a cruel murderer or a petty thief. It seems incomprehensible that war criminals and cheaters can all be forgiven if they are truly sorry for their actions and beg God to forgive them. However, to be forgiven by God does not mean that God will take away any consequences of one's sin. Whoever has committed a murder and asks God to forgive the crime still has to face the police and the judges. Otherwise one's remorse is worth nothing. And whoever steals and thinks that after confession everything is OK is mistaken. Only after one gives back the stolen object or its equivalent value is one's confession good. Forgiveness in confession is not like an automatic machine, nor can forgiveness be earned. When God forgives our sins, he wants to restore the relationship between himself and us. The new beginning with God must be followed by a new beginning between the persons involved.

SUBMIT

52

Why Believe?

Why should we believe in God?

SENDER: Will, 14

RESPONDER: Christina Riecke

You should believe in God because he believes in you. You are his idea, his image, his child. You belong together. God misses you when you are not with him. He searches for you and gives you advice. God has given you your life, and someday he will ask you what you did with that life. God has given you all your successes. Without God you would be alone. To trust in God is the greatest thing you can do.

SUBMIT

God Loves All People

YOUR QUESTION: It is said that God loves all people without exception. He forgives our sins. But if someone does not believe in God, God will not let that person enter his kingdom. Now, if God loves all people, why should he deny those who do not believe the forgiveness of their sins and their entrance into heaven?

SENDER: Heather, 15

RESPONDER: Monika Deitenbeck

God does not force anyone to come to him. He did not make us puppets but made us true counterparts who of their own free will love him or reject him. It is said that God in Christ reconciled the world to himself and willed that all people should be helped. We are no doubt curious how God will accomplish that, but we will see in the end that God will be greater than all else.

SUBMIT

Father without Mother?

How does God happen to have a son since he had no wife?

Katie, age unknown

Brother Paul Terwitte

No, God did not have a wife and God did not "happen" to have a son. Jesus has always been with the Father just as the Holy Spirit has. The three are one God. Their love for one another is similar to that of a happy family. Through this love they created the world. Later Jesus became human by the Father through the Holy Spirit. Jesus is much more than a miracle worker or a good person among many others. Because of him, other people also exist. And all these people are brothers and sisters to this one Son, Jesus.

God in Creation?

YOUR QUESTION: My father says he goes to the forest when he is searching for God. Does God speak through his creation?

SENDER: Miriana, 15

RESPONDER: Christina Riecke

I think that in one way all creation, be it nature, animals, flowers, or all the different people, shows how creative God is. Yes, creation can inspire awe and can make us think and can tell us some things about God. For example, very few people, on seeing a rainbow, think of chemistry class in grade nine or say, "Oh, it's a mixture of water and light." Most people are somehow touched by this sign and realize that behind this symbol in the sky is surely more....On the other hand, I think that a tree is really just a tree and, by far, not God; a star is a star, a "lamp" that God hung in the sky. Creation can be an indication of the Creator, but it is not God himself. You find God when you talk to him directly.

SUBMIT

Just God

YOUR QUESTION: If I hear a special voice in my heart, how can I be sure it is really God?

SENDER: Caitlin, 14

RESPONDER: Brother Paul Terwitte

Do you realize that you are not talking to yourself? We can be trained to think along certain lines. Our pictures of God are greatly influenced by our culture. However, there is one thing that people have experienced again and again through the centuries. God is present, even if I do not think about him. He calls himself in the Bible, "I am who I am" (Exod 3:14). Memories, stories, pictures that we carry in our minds are somehow invented by us. But through all this, faith begins and you know: "This is not my creation. It is made by God."

SUBMIT

Faith in a Coma

Can God continue to live in the heart of a person who is in a coma without leaving the person even for a second, or does that person have to begin anew his/her relationship with God? What if, after being in a coma, the person has lost faith and decides to live as an atheist?

SENDER: Megan, 17

RESPONDER: Marcus C. Leitschuh

I take comfort in Jesus' reasurring words, "I will be with you always." When God raised Jesus from the dead, he showed us that God will not leave a person alone, especially when one is sick. As long as a person is free he/she can decide for a life with or without God. Frequently it happens that a serious illness causes a person to have very different thoughts about life and, consequently, that person can have a change of personality. God does not desert that person, but the person is forced to find a way back to truth. He has to accept the fact that he has been ill and that his life will continue differently. He must realize that, in spite of his feeling of emptiness, God is still with him to help him. Hopefully, he will experience a new beginning.

In Seven Days

SENDER: Beth, 14

RESPONDER: Monika Deitenbeck

God created the world. He guided humanity and let humans experience his power. The ancient Bible writers were basically saying, "All you people who think that the sun, the moon, and the stars are gods who control our lives, think again! *God* made these lights for the sky." The Bible writers were trying to make us understand that God is the Lord, the Creator, and that we can rejoice over his creation. This holds true even today. These early writers did not intend to make a scientific report about how the universe was created. Instead, they wanted us to understand that God created the world with purpose and love.

SUBMIT

Football God

SENDER: Mike, 10

RESPONDER: Marcus C. Leitschuh

In some religions the people believe that there is a special god for everything that happens in the world: rain, lovers, or war. The ancient Romans and other "nature nations" had that belief. Judaism, Christianity, and Islam are called "monotheistic religions" because they believe in one God for all conditions, so God can appropriately be called the God of football. This does not mean that he enters the game or gets involved in the decision making. In the beginning of creation God made the earth for us. That means he is not responsible for wars that human beings begin or continue. Nor is God responsible for a bad pass in football. But I am sure that he is happy if we love the sport and play fair.

SUBMIT

In Spite Of

YOUR QUESTION: Why did God create the world the way it is even though he knew that eventually it would collapse?

SENDER: Matthias, 22

RESPONDER: Brother Paul Terwitte

I ask God that question, too, sometimes. But seriously, I can explain it only this way. God must have believed that people would freely use their ability to love. Without freedom it would not be true love. Sorry to say that humans do not understand this as God's way. To atone for humanity's mistakes, God through Jesus took upon himself the sufferings created because of humanity's misunderstanding of God's plan.

SUBMIT

Is There a God?

How did people first learn that there is a God?

SENDER: Rachel, 14

RESPONDER: Monika Deitenbeck

Why do people fall in love? We feel a longing for the other sex, and the person of the other sex feels a longing for us. This is how we find each other, and sometimes we must learn the hard way to live together peacefully.

There is another kind of longing in us: our longing for God, who in turn longs for us. God searches for us, and we may go in search of him. Eventually he will arrive.

SUBMIT

With God in Harmony

YOUR QUESTION: What can we do to be and remain in harmony with God?

SENDER: Carsten, 16

RESPONDER: Brother Paul Terwitte

Have the courage to consider yourself God's creature. This courage is also called humility. In Latin that word is *humilitas,* which contains the word *humus.* Whoever lives in harmony with God knows that the end of human life is death—and God who saves one from death calls one back to new life. Whoever lives according to this knowledge will test all their actions to make sure that they serve the people who live in the world. That person will attribute good deeds to God and make sure that selfishness will not spoil them.

SUBMIT

For All People?

Does God really care about all people?

SENDER:

Lauren, 13

RESPONDER:

Monika Deitenbeck

Yes, he does! No human person enters this world who is not loved by God, who is not wanted or treasured by God. God wants all people to find a full life. Jesus came to help us. He surprised us by treating people differently from the way most of us treat them. He was especially close and loving to those who were considered impossible to love: the fallen away, the rejected, the shockingly deformed people, those who were called godless and rejected. He was seriously criticized for doing that. The pious people had not expected God to act in that way. But Jesus showed us that this is God's way.

SUBMIT

Why?

YOUR QUESTION: Why does God allow many things?

SENDER: Ashley, 14

RESPONDER: Brother Paul Terwitte

God sees the world as a whole. When things go well for people, they ask very few questions. Only when things go wrong with them do they ask: "How can God let this happen?"

I have become accustomed to asking myself in all situations, "Where is God acting here?" I am thinking of a terrible accident and of how the victim in the midst of suffering is led with Jesus into a new life. If I am completely downhearted because someone has disappointed me, I ask God to be as near to me as he was to Jesus in the Garden of Olives. You see, I believe that God is with us in all circumstances.

SUBMIT

YOUR QUESTION: How did God create the world?

SENDER: Drake, 14

RESPONDER: Brother Paul Terwitte

The way God created the world is similar to the way people create love. The word "creation" is a bit misleading here. It makes us think of architects, engineers, and master builders.

I prefer think of creation as an act of love, a miracle that we can't really investigate with scientific devices. Suddenly, creation just happened, and the world, the greatest of God's creations, came into existence. Through the will of God not only Time and Space were created, but also human beings who can love and respect that creation, just as God does.

This answer is probably not satisfying, because it does not respond to our thirst for a scientific explanation of creation. God's greatness and power are so tremendous that no engineer or scientist could ever be able to analyze them.

SUBMIT

Who?

YOUR QUESTION: Was God human?

SENDER: Patrick, 14

RESPONDER: Monika Deitenbeck

Amazingly, Yes! To be more precise: God remained in heaven and simultaneously became human on earth as Jesus, God-Made-Flesh. He did this out of love for humankind, to search for his lost people and to save them from the power of death. Jesus lived our life and died our death and rose from the dead. He defeated death, the devil, sin, and hell and then returned to God in heaven. But he left his Spirit, God-in-us, Jesus-in-us. In technical terms we call this the Trinity: God the Father, God the Son, God the Holy Spirit.

SUBMIT

YOUR QUESTION: Does God really exist?

SENDER: Rachel, 14

RESPONDER: Brother Paul Terwitte

As truly as you and I exist, God also exists. You, too, are more than what can be seen. Even if you explain much about yourself, people still do not know who you really are. The reality of God is similar to that. You see flowers, you notice what love is, and you marvel at the way the world functions. Those are all ways in which God reveals himself to you. But to realize that God is really there for you, that he truly loves you and all the people in the world—that is where faith begins.

SUBMIT

No Faith Anymore

YOUR QUESTION: Why do so many people no longer believe in God?

SENDER: Nora, 11

RESPONDER: Christina Riecke

Personally I do not believe your observation is correct. Maybe it is true that in some places fewer and fewer people attend religious services or are members of a church. First of all, I believe that many people are searching for God and are asking themselves important spiritual questions about the meaning of life, about eternity, about forgiveness, and about redemption. Fifteen years ago when I myself became a Christian, I thought that prayer was something old fashioned, for old people, or for country folks. Today people in talk shows and books speak about contemplation, meditation, prayer, the monastic era, and similar prayer topics. God is in general conversation. We have not nearly exhausted these topics. In the second place, your observation, seen from a global perspective, is not correct. In Africa, Asia, and Latin America the churches are growing. This is also true in countries like India, even though the Christians there are in the minority and have long been persecuted. I believe that God believes in us and is not yet finished with us.

SUBMIT

Does God Believe?

Does God believe only in those who believe in him?

SENDER: Lauren, 13

RESPONDER: Brother Paul Terwitte

With each new day, God patiently tries to be with each person. For me that is the most beautiful reason to believe in God. All are wanted by him. All are searched for by him. I always feel welcome in God's presence. He does not condemn or prefer anyone over another. Maybe you can imagine how it hurts when we put off respondng to God's love. Oh, you have waited for me so long! Why didn't I pray to you before now, or make important decisions with you in mind? How glad I am that in spite of my being late, I may still come to you.

SUBMIT

All That God Wanted

YOUR QUESTION: Did God get everything he hoped for from us?

SENDER: Rachel, 14

RESPONDER: Brother Paul Terwitte

No, God has not always gotten from humans what he wanted, but he has always given the guidance that helps us. God gave us commandments, but we have disobeyed them again and again. This saddens God, who in the beginning surely pictured the world differently. Even today God is waiting for people to realize how much he is living with them. Neither did God receive back what he has modeled for us in Christ. People must learn to understand that they can forgive, that they can love, that they should respond to God's love. Each day God blesses and empowers the world. It is up to us to accept his blessing and power so that he can receive from us what he always intended—our love.

YOUR QUESTION: How did people find out that there is a God?

SENDER: Patrick, 14

RESPONDER: Marcus C. Leitschuh

People have always believed in someone or something: in gods, in causes, in explanations about the beginning of the world. But eventually God made himself known to us humans. He did this, for example, in the concrete life story of the Jews, whom he freed from slavery. People have always used this story to prove that God frees his people. He made himself known in the burning bush and gave his name: "I am who I am. I will always be with you from the beginning of the world to its end." This explanation convinced humans that God is the source of everything and that he truly wishes to help us.

SUBMIT

Faith from Childhood On

YOUR QUESTION: Why does the Lord make believing so difficult for some, even when they try to be faithful? I don't understand why people of faith have doubts and misunderstandings. Does God only want those who find it easier to believe in him? No wonder the Christian community shrinks day by day.

SENDER: Katharina, 23

RESPONDER: Christina Riecke

I would like to tell you only this much: I wish very much that in your heart you could be happy with God.

I am convinced that Jesus is very near to those who doubt, who search, and who question. Think about how he himself asked the worst of all human questions: "My God, my God, why have you forsaken me?" (Matt 27:46). This brings him very close to all who think God has forsaken them.

One more thing! I know people from Christian and non-Christian families who have completely lost their faith. And there are those from Christian and non-Christian families for whom faith in God is very easy. Neither the first group nor the second has life essentially easier. I myself have gone through many transitions. I know only one thing: Jesus always listens to my prayers.

SUBMIT

Being an Atheist

Is it very bad not to believe in God?

SENDER: Dan, 16

RESPONDER: Marcus C. Leitschuh

If there is a wonderful young man in your school, is it bad if you do not like him? This is, of course, not a very simple comparison, but in such cases you may have the feeling that you might miss something without him. Maybe later you are even sorry that you did not try to make friends with him. Many can live without believing in God. You won't live a longer or shorter life; you won't have more or less money; and you will probably also be happy. But you will miss the greatest gift that is ready for us in eternity.

SUBMIT

The Way

How does God show me the way?

SENDER: Jacob, 17

RESPONDER: Christina Riecke

I realize that God often speaks to me through other people. They inspire me, criticize me, or encourage me. They give me new ideas. They point out to me things that I overlooked. God also gives me certain impulses, ideas that suddenly are in my head and surprise me, thoughts that were more God's thoughts than mine. This happens especially when I am reading the Bible, praying, or singing. In the stories of Jesus and in his teachings I find very concrete directions of how I should live my life. There are also many incidental events that can provide direction.

One more thing: in my workplace we often experience stress because someone cannot find a key. We all search for it and look in the most unusual places, even in the refrigerator. Finally the key is discovered by someone who calmly searches in the usual places. In your search for God's way, don't be nervous, hectic, or even fearful. See what God can put right in front of you!

SUBMIT

An Image of God

YOUR QUESTION: What does God look like? Why does the Bible say, "Don't create an image of God," and then constantly talk about God in images?

SENDER: Rebecca, 18

RESPONDER: Christina Riecke

You are right. The Bible is especially picturesque when it speaks of God. It calls him light, rock, king, shepherd, source, father, judge, living one, mother. Love may use all powers of imagination to express who God is.

What the Bible wants to prevent humans from doing is to pin God down to a particular image, because that would limit God. Therefore, no single country can draw God on its flag. No skin color, no sex, no age is given. If God were only an old man, he would be very limited. No surprises about God would happen any more—for God would not be God.

SUBMIT

76

Can God Prevent Bad Things Happening?

YOUR QUESTION: Hi! First of all! Yesterday I was asked by a good friend why God did not prevent the birth of Hitler. I had no answer for him...so I am turning to you for the answer.

SENDER: Alison, 15

RESPONDER: Marcus C. Leitschuh

When a new student comes into class the teacher must always give him a chance, even if the student has a disciplinary record. People aren't born dictators, but begin their lives with God's blessing. What they make of their lives depends on themselves, their families, and society. God guides a person's life, but doesn't want to dictate it. It might seem that God is either naïve or taking a risk that people might refuse his love and do evil deeds, as Hitler did. This is partly true. God doesn't want dictators and murderers to die. But neither does he want ot force people to be good. Whatever their background, with God's help all people can change. If a person doesn't change, God won't interfere. I think it's great that we don't have to worry about God interfering with our actions every day. The Bible says you cannot know the direction of the wind or the child growing in the mother's womb. Nor can you know the mind of God who does everything (see Eccl 11:5).

SUBMIT

World Catastrophe

How are natural catastrophes like the tsunami in Southeast Asia possible in spite of God's love for humanity? He has created the world, so why then did he not prevent it?

SENDER: Martin, 15

RESPONDER: Marcus C. Leitschuh

In Genesis (8:21–22) it is written that Noah thanked God after the flood. God was pleased about that and said to Noah: "I will never again curse the ground because of humankind, for the inclination of the human heart is evil from youth; nor will I ever again destroy every living creature as I have done. As long as the earth endures, seedtime and harvest, cold and heat, summer and winter, day and night, shall not cease."

Then the rainbow appeared as a sign of God's faithfulness. This promise still holds true even today. God will not punish, even if he has to see that some people remain wicked. A flood like the one in Southeast Asia is not God's work. It is not a catastrophe caused by God. It is a natural catastrophe. In the millions of years of the existence of the earth there have been thousands of such catastrophes. Through them we can see how small we are in comparison to these natural powers, so let us not act as if we have power over these natural happenings. To know that we are in God's hands along with the rest of his creation—that is an attitude of living by which we can keep calm, even during the worst experiences of nature. God's covenant with Noah still holds true today.

SUBMIT

Does God Know What He Wants?

YOUR QUESTION: Why does God ask Abraham in Genesis 22 to sacrifice his son? Is that not in contrast to 1 Kings 3:26 and Jeremiah 32:35 and other biblical passages? They show that sacrificing a child is against God's will. Could Abraham have only *thought* that God demanded this of him?

SENDER: Julia, 16

RESPONDER: Christina Riecke

This is a difficult story. Some time ago I made a beautiful discovery: When Isaac asked his father on the way to the altar of sacrifice, "The fire and the wood are here, but where is the lamb for a burnt offering?" Isaac said, "God himself will provide the lamb for a burnt offering, my son" (Gen 22:7–8). I believe that Abraham did not just want to avoid answering his son's question but truly meant what he said. From the depth of his faith he could say "God himself will provide the lamb for a burnt offering." It was not God's way to accept a sacrificed child, and that is how the story ended. Isaac is not sacrificed. Instead Abraham finds a lamb. In Israel child sacrifices were forbidden.

One more thought. Jesus, the Son of God, was also called "Lamb of God." Jesus does not demand sacrifices, does not make sacrifices, but offers himself in our place. And God is a God of life and resurrects Jesus from the dead.

SUBMIT

THREE
WHO IS JESUS?

Aggression, Resurrection, Demons, Questions,
Healing, Marriage, Disciples, Children, Cross,
Listening, Sex, Death, Water, Miracles

Jesus

YOUR QUESTION: Did Jesus really live?

SENDER: Adam, 16

RESPONDER: Christina Riecke

Yes, Jesus really lived. I believe that his life, his words, his deeds, his death and resurrection are really true. They are all historical events that took place nearly two thousand years ago in Jerusalem, in Israel, which can be found on a map. His was not a toy crucifix or fake "movie" blood. Jesus died a true death through the ancient Roman method of crucifixion and suffered real pain and agony. His world-famous Sermon on the Mount, his deeds of love, his nearness to human beings are not the invention of some author. Many witnesses of his deeds remembered them and told us what Jesus said and did. It was very clear to them that Jesus showed God's love in a unique way and that he is our Savior, who saves us from eternal damnation.

SUBMIT

Miracles

YOUR QUESTION: How did Jesus manage to cure a blind man?

SENDER: Natalie, 14

RESPONDER: Monika Deitenbeck

Yes, Jesus could heal the blind, the lame, and other sick people because he came to bring salvation to the world, to remove us from the power of death, to unite us again with God, and to open the gates of heaven for us. God's concern is not for the good of our soul alone. He is interested in the entire human person—body and soul, heart and spirit, hide and hair. He is interested in our whole well-being.

In God's new world all tears are wiped away. Death will no longer exist, nor suffering nor crying. The last book of the Bible tells us that, and Jesus often talked about it. Because God wanted this healthy world, he sent Jesus. He does signs and wonders, but no magic acts or showmanship. All his actions are expressions and proof of his divine power and a foretaste of God's next world, where everything will be new. Jesus can open our eyes to God's message and the promise of his new world.

SUBMIT

Jesus on the Cross

YOUR QUESTION: How do we know that Jesus died on the cross?

SENDER: Maria, 15

RESPONDER: Monika Deitenbeck

Jesus' death is verified many times in the New Testament, and it has also been told to us outside of the Bible orally through tradition. For example, a caricature of the second century was found, a cross with the head of a donkey on it. At the foot of the cross is written in Greek "Alexander adores his God." Dying on a cross was the most humiliating form of execution, used to punish the worst criminals during the time of Jesus. There were crosses everywhere. It seems incredible that God allowed this to happen to Jesus. And yet Jesus, God-made-man, dies on the cross. With that he proved for all time that he identified with the lowest class of society and did not let himself be separated from them.

SUBMIT

Died of His Own Free Will

SENDER: Daniel, 16

RESPONDER: Brother Paul Terwitte

Jesus became the victim of a plot, but he did not try to escape from it. He spoke openly and courageously about his Father in heaven. It was sad that not everyone could accept that. People preferred to condemn a person in the name of God and exclude him from society. Jesus proved that God's strength lies in a different direction. With God's support we can help other people to start anew. With God's support we can help others lead a good life. And with God's help we can bear any suffering for the sake of envious or deluded people.

SUBMIT

Were the Disciples Cowards?

YOUR QUESTION: Couldn't Jesus disciples have defended him better when he was attacked?

SENDER: Sam, 14

RESPONDER: Christina Riecke

I asked myself the same question when I read about Jesus' arrest. But when I place myself in the position of the disciples, I can imagine that they were afraid and only thought of a way to get safely out of the situation. That's why they ran away.

In addition to this, when one of the disciples drew a sword to defend Jesus and cut off the ear of one of the soldiers, Jesus could not approve of that violent action. He immediately healed the soldier and said, "Put away your sword." He probably did so because he knew that his message could not be stopped and because force was never his method. He loved! He loved unto death even when he could have freed himself.

SUBMIT

YOUR QUESTION: Why did Jesus heal the soldier whose ear was cut off?

SENDER: Daniel, 16

RESPONDER: Monika Deitenbeck

Jesus knows no hatred, does not want us to use force, and even tells us to love our enemies. That is why he healed the wound that the other had inflicted on the soldier. Besides, Jesus knew that thousands of angels would protect him if he wanted them to do so. Right now his perseverance was being tested while he was being betrayed, arrested, slandered, hurt, and killed. His task was to heal the wounds between heaven and earth. He began by healing the wound of the soldier.

SUBMIT

Was Jesus a father?

Did Jesus have children?

SENDER: Julia, 15

RESPONDER: Monika Deitenbeck

No, Jesus had a very special commission from God and a limited time to fulfill it. He loved, enjoyed, suffered, supported life, family, and friends, but for three years he constantly moved without a definite home. And he knew how it would all end—while he was still young—on a cross. So this lover of life and of people, of feasts and celebrations, this dedicated person lived his special commission without wife and children.

SUBMIT

Resurrection from the Dead

YOUR QUESTION: Did Jesus really rise from the dead?

SENDER: Natasha, 14

RESPONDER: Brother Paul Terwitte

Of course! This means that Jesus became a natural human being through God, the Father, and lived here in our midst. In seeing him, people could know how God thought humans should be. Jesus existed with God as the prototype of humans before humans ever existed. On earth Jesus suffered until death. People deny the love by which they should really live. Jesus' Father in heaven raised him from the dead because Jesus loved all people in spite of their hatred. He is the new prototype for a new life in close relationship with God.

Besides, the message of the risen Savior Jesus was the first thing that was told about the Savior. Only later did people write down how he was born and relate what he did. The resurrection as an unusual experience changed everything and became documented in the history of humankind.

SUBMIT

To Draw Near to Jesus

What must I do to draw near to Jesus?

SENDER: Amanda, 18

RESPONDER: Christina Riecke

Maybe you know this children's prayer:
I am little.
My heart is pure.
No one may live there
But Jesus alone.
Speaking honestly, I never liked this prayer.
Recently my godchild said this prayer. Wondering if she liked the prayer, I asked, "What do you imagine when you say it?" And she answered, "My heart beats all day. It sounds to me as if Jesus is knocking at the door. I tell him, 'Come in. I love to have you with me.'"

I believe that Jesus is already with you. You do not have to do anything special for that to be true. But you can make a conscious effort and tell him, "I trust you. I do not want to live without you. I wish to get to know you. I would like to know who you are and what your life and death mean for me." You can start an unusual friendship.

SUBMIT

Truth or Fairy Tale?

YOUR QUESTION: How do we know that the miracle stories about Jesus are true? Weren't the stories repeated by others and each one exaggerated a little until in the end they became miracles?

SENDER: Christopher, no age indicated.

RESPONDER: Christina Riecke

My life would be very sad if each time someone told me about some wonderful event I would have to think, "This is too beautiful to be true. Such things happen only in fairy tales. This story must be invented." I do not think that way if someone tells me how he became reconciled with an enemy, how he found love, how he became well, or how he was courageous enough to do some good. If I hear some great stories I am happy, and this is the way I feel about the stories in the Bible. I am still waiting for miracles. Maybe I have overlooked some already. I have often expressed how wonderful Jesus is.

SUBMIT

Jesus as Single

YOUR QUESTION: Was Jesus married?

SENDER: Julia, 15

RESPONDER: Brother Paul Terwitte

No. Of all the things that are speculated about Jesus, this is one of the historically surest facts. He was unmarried. As a wandering preacher, he would not have been able to support a family. Besides that, it was to become clear that his love extended to all human beings. And since it is for all, each can experience it personally. This was God's purpose in sending Jesus into this world: to let each person enter into a deep relationship with him. Some people go so far as to call Jesus their bridegroom.

SUBMIT

Ascension

YOUR QUESTION: How could Jesus ascend into heaven after his death?

SENDER: Alex, 17

RESPONDER: Monika Deitenbeck

God took Jesus back to his glory. In the Old Testament the cloud has always been an expression of the presence of God. At his so-called ascension Jesus disappeared in a cloud before the eyes of his disciples. He returned to God's eternal world, heaven. Yet we can approach him any time we wish to do so. We do not need an audience, as we do to visit with the Holy Father. We can talk to Jesus any time we want to because he is with us through all eternity.

SUBMIT

Sex

YOUR QUESTION: Did Jesus have sex?

SENDER: Lisa Maria, 16

RESPONDER: Brother Paul Terwitte

No, but he was a very loving person. In the Bible it says that he touched people, embraced them, and blessed them. The Bible does not know the word "sex." It is concerned with body, soul, and spirit—becoming human, woman or man. Jesus, as man, was to live a special history. He attracted men as well as women. Prostitutes came to him. Tax collectors followed him. All his followers learned that life is more than sex, money, or selfishness. Through Jesus they came to know the meaning of the whole person.

SUBMIT

YOUR QUESTION: Why did Jesus choose only men to be his disciples?

SENDER: Lisa, 16

RESPONDER: Brother Paul Terwitte

Jesus also had women among his followers. Luke 8:3 expressly says that women followed and supported Jesus. Women were the first who heard the Easter message (Matt 27:61) and took the news to the frightened men. Women played a leading role in the continuation of the faith throughout the centuries. It may anger some people that women never occupied powerful positions. They were credible witnesses of Jesus' teaching and really lived the faith. They witnessed Jesus and helped to spread the faith.

SUBMIT

Crucifixion

Why was Jesus crucified?

SENDER: Marcel, 14

RESPONDER: Monika Deitenbeck

There are two responses: fact and meaning

Fact: The so-called "religious" people just could not believe that God really was the one whom Jesus was talking about, and so they condemned him as a blasphemer. The political leaders were afraid of Christ. They feared that the followers of Jesus would cause a political revolt against the Roman government, and they preferred to kill an innocent man rather than risk a rebellion.

Meaning: God becomes human, allows himself to be nailed to a cross, and through his death conquers hell. God dies so that the devil, sin, hell, and death may be conquered and be powerless for all eternity. The world could not be saved by human efforts alone.

SUBMIT

YOUR QUESTION: What did Jesus do before he started to preach?

SENDER: Jonathan, 16

RESPONDER: Marcus C. Leitschuh

The four evangelists write nothing about the childhood of Jesus. Mark begins with the baptism of Jesus in the Jordan. Luke and Matthew both have a long gap in the story after Jesus' birth in the stable. They only briefly relate the story about Jesus being lost and remaining in the temple teaching for three days when he and his parents were in Jerusalem. Until he was thirty years old Jesus probably worked as a carpenter with his father and studied the Torah in the synagogue as young men did in his time.

SUBMIT

Walk on Water?

Could Jesus really walk on water?

SENDER: Adam, 16

RESPONDER: Monika Deitenbeck

If God is the creator of the world, the earth, and the powers of nature; if God is Lord when he comes into the world to save it from the powers of hell; if God calls himself Jesus but still remains God even though he is also human, then it is logical that his being God and Lord could be felt while he was man. It is also logical that the power of water is subject to Jesus' divine power. Therefore, yes, Jesus as God-man could really walk across the water.

And Peter, as man, was told to do the same. He makes a surprising discovery: With my gaze on Jesus, I too can walk on water. When Peter sees the storm, he falls, but Jesus holds him tightly so that he does not drown. This also happens to us.

SUBMIT

Answer with Questions

YOUR QUESTION: Why does Jesus generally answer questions with another question?

SENDER: Chris, 19

RESPONDER: Christina Riecke

Jesus is usually interested in the person who is asking the question. He wants to know what is behind the question: What is this person doing? What are his motives and desires? Jesus does not want to answer the question superficially or too quickly. If you read these discussions (or question-and-answer dialogues) between Jesus and the questioner, you will notice that Jesus' questions often move to the true point. He looks deeper. Even if a superficial question is not bad, it is not your real goal, your happiness, your intention. Superficial topics are OK, but they are not the main idea. Your skin is not the heart, and Jesus is searching for your heart.

SUBMIT

100

Jesus

YOUR QUESTION: I have a disability. Some people told me that God wanted to punish me or my family. They said that Jesus shed his blood for my sins. I was angry. I do not need a Jesus to suffer for me. I want to live happily.

SENDER: Vicky, 17

RESPONDER: Brother Paul Terwitte

I can hardly believe that there are people who refer to your handicap as being a punishment from God. They are talking nonsense. God does not want suffering. Rather he is suffering with you. He sends you the Holy Spirit to strengthen you. As far as Jesus is concerned, he has shed his blood for us. Jesus' suffering is God's redemptive power for us. He loves us even when no one else can lead us from results of sin to peace. Jesus accepted his sufferings in the name of God. Even today, through his resurrection, Jesus takes us into a new community with God to enjoy eternal happiness.

SUBMIT

Jesus, Son of God, and Free Will

Did Jesus have free will to decide for or against God? Was it clear from the beginning that he is the Son of God? But if he was human like us he must have had a free choice.

SENDER: Vera, no age given

RESPONDER: Marcus C. Leitschuh

When Jesus was baptized in the Jordan, God spoke from heaven: "This is my Son, my Beloved, with whom I am well pleased" (Matt 3:17). This acknowledgement was meant for Jesus, and for all people. Genesis (1:27) states that we are created "in the image of God." Deuteronomy (14:1) states that we are all "children of God." This means God's will is evident in our biological parents, who tell each child, "You are wanted." Jesus was sent into the world without a biological father so that people would understand this. He was special, but he also had to accept the difficulties of being truly human. Early Christians did not quite understand this tension between being God and human and discussed it just as we are now, asking questions just like yours. A Bishops' Council in AD 325 formulated a statement about the "essential quality" of Christ and God. The Council of Chalcedon (AD 451) added that Jesus was both "essentially equal" to humans and still "true God." I can't tell you how willingly Jesus fulfilled his Father's command, but we can see how his actions benefit us when we live according to God's will.

SUBMIT

Free Will?

YOUR QUESTION: We human beings have free will but it was already prophesied that Jesus was to die on the cross. So didn't Pontius Pilate and all who participated in the crucifixion do the will of God? In that case, were they guilty of Jesus' death? Didn't it have to happen?

SENDER: Toby, 22

RESPONDER: Brother Paul Terwitte

God allows people to act according to their own decisions. On the Mount of Olives Jesus said to Peter, who wanted to defend him, "Do you think that I cannot appeal to my Father, and he will at once send me more than twelve legions of angels? But how then would the scriptures be fulfilled, which say it must happen in this way?" (Matt 26:53–54), which means that everything is happening according to a hard-to-understand logic. Judas and Pilate were caught up in that logic. And as is the case with all evil, on the one hand they could choose between acting or not; on the other hand they were limited in knowledge. How much personal guilt either one had is difficult to say. In my opinion, however, in both cases the guilt of humankind in eliminating God from our lives seems to be clear.

SUBMIT

FOUR
WHAT DOES THE
BIBLE SAY?

Egypt, Apostles, Adam and Eve, Demons,
Jonah and the Whale, Justice, Virgin Mary, Red Sea,
Contradictions, Discipleship, Pentecost, Sex,
Old and New Testaments, the Word

Divided Waters

YOUR QUESTION: How could Moses divide the sea?

SENDER: Kevin, 17

RESPONDER: Monika Deitenbeck

Because God gave him the power to do it! Repeatedly God has called certain individuals to perform special tasks. Moses was called for such a task. In the name of God he was to lead his people out of slavery. God himself accompanied his people and gave Moses leadership qualities. Moses was a human being with all his weaknesses, and he also had speech defects. But being called by God, he obeyed, so nothing could block his way, not even the Red Sea. God always finds a way.

SUBMIT

The Bible

YOUR QUESTION: What does it mean "to take the Bible seriously"?

SENDER: Charles, 15

RESPONDER: Christina Riecke

What does reading the Bible mean for me? It is a voice in my life. I decided that it has something important to tell me. It has authority over me, one that can answer my questions well. It does not dictate. It has no empty pages, just like I myself am not an empty page. I need the Bible because it tells stories that I would not hear anywhere else. It contains original thoughts that I would never find any other way. For example, it tells expressly about being awakened from death while our human experience goes only as far as death. It urges us to maintain peace when we so quickly think that there is no alternative but war. It is constantly asking for more love while I think I try enough to love others. For me the Bible is the best teacher, critic, consoler, and storyteller.

SUBMIT

Fiery Tongues

YOUR QUESTION: Why didn't the people catch on fire when the fiery tongues came down on them at Pentecost?

SENDER: Kevin, 16

RESPONDER: Christina Riecke

The participants in the Pentecost experience say that this impressive experience was like the rushing of the wind and like fire. It felt like fire. Maybe it felt like the experience of falling in love. You think your heart is burning. It doesn't physically burn—but you are like "fire and flame." Pentecost is happening to you today when you get enthusiastic about God. You can truly become "warm around the heart."

SUBMIT

Poetry or Truth?

Is the Bible a fairytale?

SENDER: Diane, 8

RESPONDER: Marcus C. Leitschuh

"Don't tell me stories," people say to those who lie. A story is not really a lie. Behind each story some truth is hidden. The Bible is a book written by men in such a way that it could and would be read by people. The stories were written in such a way that readers would be attracted to read and understand them. The stories had to be exciting enough to appeal to readers and listeners. Many of the writers of the Bible therefore used a story structure that was used by other storytellers. That is how it happened that some Bible stories are constructed in the same way as fairytales or fables. And the method was also patterned in reverse—some authors of fairytales used the Bible method of storytelling because their stories were so fascinating.

Each fairytale says, "Behind our story lies a message." In the Bible this message is "God is with us. He is the foundation of our life. We will live with him forever."

SUBMIT

To Take It Literally

YOUR QUESTION: Can the Bible be taken literally?

SENDER: Christina, 13

RESPONDER: Christina Riecke

I agree that at times the Bible is irritatingly complicated or even unintelligible. But I read on, swallow, and notice how it satisfies me. And I experience how the Bible speaks to me, even literally a few times. For example: one of our Indian godchildren in our church community is named Venda. Her life story is written in English, and in the story it is explained that "Venda" means "not wanted." One morning we read the Bible in the Indian language: "The Lord is my shepherd, I shall not want" (Psalm 23). "Nothing shall be lacking for me." "I shall not want." We all looked at each other and said, "Venda, do you know what your name really means? Nothing will be wanting to you. You are taken care of. The Lord is your Shepherd."

SUBMIT

Virgin and Mother

How could a virgin become pregnant?

SENDER: Chris, 17

RESPONDER: Monika Deitenbeck

When God created the universe, he created it out of nothing. When he wanted to become human to save lost humanity from death, he looked for a place. It sounds strange, but out of love for us God acted in a strange manner and thought of a unique idea: He looked for a person who would receive him and found Mary, who said, "I am the handmaid of the Lord." Her word was enough, and she carried the Son of God. This is how the true God also became true man, in Mary's womb. Only God can accomplish that. Because he is God he is powerful, and because he loves humankind he became very human.

SUBMIT

Pregnant without Man?

How could Mary become pregnant without a husband?

SENDER: Jordan, 15

RESPONDER: Brother Paul Terwitte

This story is to be understood as a second act of creation. It is said about the first one: "In the beginning when God created the heavens and the earth, the earth was a formless void and darkness covered the face of the deep, while a wind from God swept over the face of the waters" (Gen 1:1–2). The reason? To create humans. God wanted to be loved by someone on the earth. Sorry to say that humanity used its liberty to love itself more than to love God. Now God again exerted his power and the Holy Spirit overshadowed Mary (see Luke 1:35) and Jesus, the new man, was created not through the power of man but through the power of the Spirit.

SUBMIT

Demons

YOUR QUESTION: Were the apostles truly able to drive out demons?

SENDER: Angela, 15

RESPONDER: Monika Deitenbeck

Yes, they were able to do so because they prayed in the name of Jesus to overcome the power of evil. Jesus conquered hell, death, and the darkness of all evil. Therefore the apostles could drive out demons because Jesus was the stronger.

SUBMIT

Old and
New Testaments

YOUR QUESTION: Why is there an Old and New
Testament?

SENDER: Annie, 14

RESPONDER: Christina Riecke

The entire Bible is really a collection of many
smaller books: some longer, some shorter; some full of
history, some full of stories; some in prose, some in
poetic form. The books of the Old Testament are not
invalid or old-fashioned; they are simply older in time.
You could call it the First Testament. The New
Testament fulfills especially the promises and
prophecies of the Old Testament in its main character,
Jesus. Jesus brings something entirely new but he does
not start "from scratch." He takes seriously the
tradition of the Old Testament and expresses it more
radically in many instances or fulfills its promises.

The two parts of the Bible make one unique book.
It is wise to read them both.

SUBMIT

To Follow Jesus

YOUR QUESTION: Why did the first disciples of Jesus have to give up everything to follow Jesus?

SENDER: Evan, 15

RESPONDER: Marcus C. Leitschuh

Jesus gathered his disciples mainly from around Lake Genesareth, and most of them were fishermen. The Bible says that they left everything, but their following of Jesus meant that they stayed mostly around the lake. They could conveniently return to their friends and families. They did not have to break off all contacts, which would have been a very difficult command for Jesus to make. Still he said: "Whoever loves father or mother more than me is not worthy of me." Whoever is for Jesus must see everything with new eyes. Everything takes on new value when Jesus and the kingdom of God become the most precious possessions.

The demand "to leave everything" can also be read as a sign: whoever follows Jesus, whoever wants to work near him and for him—for that person there is nothing more important. Following Jesus cannot be done "on the side." As Christians, we have all been called to follow Christ every day and to give up whatever keeps us from living with Christ.

SUBMIT

Four Gospels

Why are there four different Gospels?

SENDER: Tim, 14

RESPONDER: Brother Paul Terwitte

Remember that only after the resurrection of Jesus did people begin to ask: "Who is this Jesus?" "Where did he come from?" "What did he do?" By the third century there existed about twenty-five different gospels, and many were copied from each other. During the Council of Toledo the church decided that the four texts of Matthew, Mark, Luke, and John were closest to the message about the death and resurrection of Jesus and that these gospels showed best who Jesus really was.

SUBMIT

Grown Old?

YOUR QUESTION: Isn't the Bible much too old? Shouldn't we write a new Bible that is more modern?

SENDER: Jacob, 16

RESPONDER: Monika Deitenbeck

The message of the Bible can never become too old for us. Maybe if we have a very old translation, the language seems quaint. Since the Bible was originally written in Hebrew and Greek, it must be translated into the languages that are spoken today for the readers of today's world. The content of the Bible is such that it can be experienced anew with each translation. We can then notice how near to our lives its content is. It is also very helpful to read the Bible with other members of our community. We can ask questions and understand many things better than we did before.

SUBMIT

Sex and the Bible

YOUR QUESTION: Does the Bible contain anything about sex, relationships, and love?

SENDER: Dorothy, 18

RESPONDER: Christina Riecke

Yes, certainly! Stories of this kind are told very openly. Also topics like revenge, abuse, fraud, envy, and conflict are discussed as they truly exist and are not kept as secrets. The Bible tells about life as it really happens and, more than that, it tells about how life could be.

Many stories and ideas in the Bible mention something about love. They tell about the love among family members, friendships of men and women, women's groups, neighbors helping each other, and even love of enemies.

The Bible also includes stories about the love between a husband and a wife. It was God's idea that the two should complement each other. Both are responsible for life on earth, both should become one in heart and soul. No one should break the promise of love.

SUBMIT

Navel

YOUR QUESTION: Did Adam have a navel?

SENDER: Nick, 31

RESPONDER: Brother Paul Terwitte

Of course, just as all humans do. Adam means "human." The Bible sings an important song about the origin of humans: they come from God. Whether the first human came from a one-cell creature or from the monkey, that one did not happen to come from genes but came to live by the will of God. In any case, the Bible does not speak scientifically about navels or ribs. It simply means to say: Don't consider yourself the center of the world just because you are the only creature who has an intellect and a will. You have the power to understand, so you are more than just flesh: be a partner with God. (And God does not have a navel!)

SUBMIT

Swallowed

YOUR QUESTION: How can we imagine that a whale swallowed a human being and then spat him out on the land?

SENDER: Courtney, 14

RESPONDER: Christina Riecke

Speaking honestly, I could never imagine this really happening. But at the beginning of this year I observed my friend's first pregnancy and birth of her child. To imagine that this little baby swims for months in a liquid, grows, eats, and somehow knows that "out there" people are expecting him to come—this sounds strange. The experiences of being born and seeing the light, breathing, crying, looking around, being hungry, and smiling are also truly marvelous. Since then I can imagine the story of Jonah. God is ingenious, I think. He was "with" Jonah as he was with this newly born child. God is ingenious in your life also.

SUBMIT

YOUR QUESTION: How is God going to achieve justice?

SENDER: Micah, 13

RESPONDER: Christina Riecke

The weak will become strong, the hungry satisfied, those driven away will be welcomed, and those tired of life will come alive. Children will be taken seriously, and adults will laugh at themselves. The oppressed will be given rights, and refugees and homeless will get lovely rooms. Slaves will lead the dance. Those ridiculed will tell good jokes. The dumb will sing. The sad people will become as happy as clowns. The lords will pour the pure wine for everyone. The rich can finally look into everyone's eyes, even their own.

Sinners will become holy, just, and good and will not need to hide. No one will be afraid, and no one will cry because justice will be pronounced. Those who were enemies will be reconciled. Sins will be forgiven. Everything will be new.

SUBMIT

Belief in the Bible?

YOUR QUESTION: Are we directly unfaithful if we cannot accept the Bible completely because it has so many seeming contradictions?

SENDER: Laura, 17

RESPONDER: Christina Riecke

I would not say, "I believe in the Bible unconditionally." I believe in *God;* I trust Jesus; and faith tells me that the Holy Spirit resides in me. Reading the Bible helps me to strengthen my faith and trust in God. Occasionally I shake my head in "disbelief" when I read the Bible, but I take my questions and doubts to Jesus. Sometimes I "have to chew on" what I read in the Bible and it is not easy to swallow, but reading the Bible is always an experience I find satisfying. Some of the differences can be explained, new ideas are added, and others are unimportant. Believe, trust, and ask questions; keep on searching, reading, checking, and making new discoveries—they all belong together.

SUBMIT

YOUR QUESTION: Did God also create the wicked in the world?

SENDER: Marvin, 14

RESPONDER: Monika Deitenbeck

No. The reports of creation (Genesis 1, 2) in the Bible do not leave a doubt: everything that God created was planned and was very good. However, the tempter and the temptation were also present. How? From where? Why? These questions are not answered, but one thing is clear: human beings will always be confronted with definite choices. Do I yield to the temptation or do I trust in God? It is also true that God wants what is best for me and that he looks after me and gives me what I need. But the consequences result from my choices.

SUBMIT

Predestination

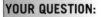

YOUR QUESTION: The letter to the Romans (8:30) says, "And those whom he predestined he also called; and those whom he called he also justified." Does this mean that God has already chosen the people whom he wants in heaven? Maybe I am one he has not chosen?

SENDER: M., 14

RESPONDER: Christina Riecke

I understand this verse to be a verification of the call to holiness for those who have actually experienced it. Paul, who had experienced God's call, wrote this passage and wanted to encourage others who had experienced God's call to trust God, meaning: God does not take anything back that he has previously decided. This verse does not say anything about the others, the so-called non-chosen, because God wants all people to be saved and to acquire knowledge and truth. Paul writes the same message to a young man in 1 Timothy 2:4.

SUBMIT

Adam's Family

YOUR QUESTION: The Bible says that Eve had two sons. How could a family like that create a world population?

SENDER: Alison, 15

RESPONDER: Christina Riecke

I believe that the story of creation wants to tell us one thing—that this world did not accidentally fall from heaven. It is God's idea. The story of Adam and Eve stresses the fact that human beings, having the ability to live in relationships, carry out God's will. The original story of Cain and Abel shows how guilt, jealousy, and mistrust can destroy a relationship. This family history shows much, but it does not give us a complete family history. Did Eve have daughters? Did the family have neighbors? That and much more are all possible. Before all else, the Bible wishes to state that living together originates in God's creative heart.

SUBMIT

Creation Stories

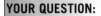

YOUR QUESTION: Why are there two creation stories? Why should I believe that everything in the Bible is true?

SENDER: Robin, 14

RESPONDER: Marcus C. Leitschuh

Genesis contains two texts about the beginning of the world: 1:1–2:4a; and 2:4b-25. These two texts don't answer the questions "What happened?" or "How did it take place?" but rather "Who made the world?" The first text is a song that shows God's creative power divided into seven days. Each verse ends with the refrain: "And God saw that it was good. It was evening and then morning came." The original text has exactly 365 words to demonstrate that God is the Lord of all time. The question answered by the second text is "Why didn't the people created by God live as God wanted them to live?" Adam and Eve did not want to live according to God's will but wanted to be like God. But whoever "plays" God will destroy the whole world. Both stories tell us that God created all things and established the laws of nature. The sun, the stars, and humans are not God, who is more than all of these. Human beings should listen to God alone and honor him above all else.

SUBMIT

Knocking on Heaven's Door?

YOUR QUESTION: It is mentioned in many places in the Bible that the door to heaven is very narrow and that only a few will enter through it. Then again it is preached that all people will go to heaven. Which statement is correct?

SENDER: Heidi, 14

RESPONDER: Brother Paul Terwitte

When Jesus speaks of the narrow gate (Luke 13:24), he wishes to draw the people's attention to the seriousness of the choice. The broad statement of getting into heaven easily may fool you. You still must make your own choice, a choice by which you may get lost. It would be even worse if you forgot that there is a God. Yet you would still have a chance because God is at the gate (Luke 15:20). God is waiting patiently for you to realize that without God wrong choices can be made too easily.

SUBMIT

FIVE

WHAT HAPPENS BETWEEN HEAVEN AND HELL?

The Sermon on the Mount, Angels, Redemption,
Fire, Judgment, Fortune, Paradise, Dying, Sin,
the Devil, Death, Condemnation

Heaven

YOUR QUESTION: Where is heaven?

SENDER: Helina, 15

RESPONDER: Monika Deitenbeck

A new Christmas song expressed it this way: "Heaven is not above; because of Jesus, it is right here. The borders have been shifted. The door is now open." God's heaven surrounds us. With Jesus, God came from heaven to earth, from eternity into time. Jesus is now the bridge between heaven and earth, between time and eternity. With Jesus we will experience heaven with our own eyes. On this earth we see him only with the eyes of our hearts.

SUBMIT

Sins of Today

YOUR QUESTION: What do we mean by "sins" today?

SENDER: Jeff, 15

RESPONDER: Christina Riecke

"Sin" is missing the goal of life, to leave God out of our lives, and the failure to love other people.

"Sins" are the evil actions you do as well as the good you neglect to do.

Maybe you know the commandments: Thou shalt not kill. Thou shalt not commit adultery. Thou shalt not steal. Thou shalt not give false witness. Read them again in the Bible. They are still important for the present time (Exod 20:1–17). Or read what Jesus says in the world-famous Sermon on the Mount (Matt 5:7), where he gives us the golden rule: "In everything, do to others as you would have them do to you" (Matt 7:12). And there are other rules stating what is good or bad. They are all concrete and timely, only sometimes a little inconvenient.

SUBMIT

Heaven's Door

How can we imagine our life with God in heaven?

SENDER: Julia, 14

RESPONDER: Marcus C. Leitschuh

Heaven is the greatest desire of all people. We hope for "paradise conditions." Many films and novels try to paint a picture of heaven. Everything is white and bright. There is talk about a large festival and of meeting deceased family members and friends. They are all pictures that suggest that we will be made as perfect as we ought to be, beautiful, and good. Especially great will be our happy, untroubled relationships with all people and with God. But so far no one has come back from heaven to show us photographs.

SUBMIT

YOUR QUESTION: What will happen to me after death?

SENDER: Will, 14

RESPONDER: Christina Riecke

Your question is, "Who is really going to tell me what to expect after death?" How can I really answer your questions when I myself have not been dead?

I have decided to trust what Jesus says in regard to this very important and big question. Read in the Bible how Jesus uses various pictures, stories, and pronouncements to tell us about life after death, about eternity, heaven, and hell; about being forsaken by God; about judgment of world history; and about the great feast with God (Matt 25; Mark 12:18–27; or Luke 16:19–31).

I trust in what Jesus says. I trust that after my death I will be with him in eternity.

SUBMIT

After Death

YOUR QUESTION: How do things continue after death?

SENDER: Gwen, 14

RESPONDER: Brother Paul Terwitte

After a life of surprises on earth, life with surprises continues after death. I imagine my death in this way: I will go through a door that will separate me forever from this world. It will certainly be a sad moment, but then happiness will begin—or, more correctly, the joy that already fills me now will continue. God wants me there. God knows me and calls me into his community. When time flies by for me now, I can feel in this life what life after death will be: time without minutes.

SUBMIT

The Last Judgment

Why does there have to be a
judgment at the end of the world?

SENDER: Sarah, 21

RESPONDER: Christina Riecke

From the way you are asking the question it seems
as if you expect God's judgment on the history of
humankind to be terrible. I would find it awful if good
and bad would be equally judged "not guilty," that is, if
God would say at the end: "Wipe out all guilt. It wasn't
all that bad." The Bible describes how Jesus the Lamb
will judge people. Jesus the Judge was also the victim.
He will tell the story of world history from the standpoint
of the victims and give them their reward. That is fair and
consoling.

Beyond that, I believe that each person can be evil
and can do evil. But I also believe that Jesus calls me to
love what God loves. I notice, however, that I don't always
follow that call and I am sorry. I know that I need God's
mercy and forgiveness.

The Bible says that those who exclude God's love
and grace from their lives and who isolate themselves
from the needs of others will themselves be isolated at
the end and be excluded from life in heaven. But whoever
gives himself to love, who trusts in Jesus, will not be
condemned. Lucky for us, God has the last word.

SUBMIT

Final Separation

YOUR QUESTION: I have heard that at the end of the world Jesus condemns the bad and accepts the good into heaven. If my friend is wicked will we be separated forever?

SENDER: Morgan, 15

RESPONDER: Christina Riecke

I often have the same dream before I speak to a group. At the gates of heaven are two groups of young people who are not allowed to enter. Some say, "You were so harsh when you talked about Jesus that we couldn't believe it." I'm shocked, since I never intended to scare them. Then the other group says, "If you had told us this was a matter of life and death, we would have taken you more seriously." I'm shocked even more. I never wanted to harm anyone, but simply to tell the truth. After I had this dream several times, I prayed, "Please let me dream the answer. How should I talk about the Last Judgment without sounding too harsh, but so that people take it seriously?" And I dreamed the same thing again! So now when anyone asks me about the Last Judgment, about heaven and hell, about separating good people from evil people, I tell them my dream and let them decide—and your friend can decide also.

SUBMIT

YOUR QUESTION: Is there really a devil?

SENDER: Greg, 16

RESPONDER: Brother Paul Terwitte

It seems that there are devils. The Bible speaks of devils or demons as forces that talk humans into abandoning God. The devil is more than some wicked power who opposes God in the battle to win humankind. What does happen again and again is that you become a stranger to yourself, a stranger who carries out a wicked action. Therefore, beware of temptation and take good care of yourself.

SUBMIT

Pretty Hot

Is there real fire in hell?

SENDER: Emma, 14

RESPONDER: Marcus C. Leitschuh

Are you really floating on "cloud 9" when you fall in love? Our language lives on images—we describe life experiences in pictures. How else can you imagine a place where we must pay for all our wicked deeds? It is uncomfortable and without luxury, the complete opposite of the pictures we have of heaven. An explanation of the pictures of heaven and hell is based on the observation of nature. Human beings learned that as one moves toward the center of the earth it becomes increasingly warm. Because this is so, that is where human beings expected hell to be. Volcanoes give a foretaste of this hell and came to be called the gates to hell. On the contrary, heaven is above us and is bright and warm.

SUBMIT

Angels

YOUR QUESTION: How many angels are there?

SENDER: Luke, 13

RESPONDER: Brother Paul Terwitte

More than can be counted, because God is constantly striving to win people for his kingdom. You must realize that angels are God's thoughts, beings of God's mind, who can quickly reach God's people. God keeps trying to make people conscious of him. He knocks at their door and asks them to do new things. He helps them understand the Bible. When people are ill, God surrounds them with his angels. In one word: God wants good things for you and wants to be close to you. He sends his angels so that you will not forget him. God often thinks of you—how often do you think of God?

SUBMIT

Life and Death

YOUR QUESTION: Why do we live at all if we have to die sometime anyway?

SENDER: Jane, 16

RESPONDER: Brother Paul Terwitte

Why do we have to die? So that we can become happy someday. Does this answer surprise you? Just imagine if you would have to awaken every morning and go to sleep every night without end. You would never grow older either. Only after you realize that everything will end some day can you truly enjoy what you now have. You will treasure life much more if you know that it happens only once and will not be repeated over and over again. Your question also suggests that you are afraid of death. I know only one answer. Death is the gate to life—to eternal life. Through this door I take all of my life experiences.

SUBMIT

Why Death

YOUR QUESTION: Why must people die?

SENDER: Kristina, age not given

RESPONDER: Christina Riecke

Often when someone asks me this question I am very quiet and cry along with the mourner. I am shocked when death suddenly interrupts the life of a person. I mourn along with those who are saying good-bye to a dying loved one. Death is the end of earthly life. We are not yet perfect, but there is more. Because God is holy and eternal he is able to gift us with eternal life. When my grandmother was dying she said, "And now I will drink a nice cup of coffee." She knew that her life would continue. Because she trusted in Jesus, she also knew that she was awaited by God. It was difficult to let her go but I was also comforted and thought, "This is how I want to die some day—full of confidence in a better future."

SUBMIT

142

Exclusive Love

YOUR QUESTION: Is it really true that after their death all atheists and all people who do not believe in Jesus Christ must forever suffer? Doesn't God love everyone in the world and forgive them?

SENDER: Christian, 16

RESPONDER: Monika Deitenbeck

Every person is a passionately loved idea of God. He wants no one to be lost. He even became a human like us, to live our life, and to die our death—and then to return in the resurrection, opening the gates of heaven. Therefore we have life both before and after death, through him, with him, and in him. But we can only go to eternity through a gate that has the form of a cross. I believe that all people will recognize this fact at the end of their lives, and go through the gate. Philippians says: "at the name of Jesus every knee should bend" (3:10), and 1 Corinthians: "God may be in all (15:28)." God will make everything right in the end. He wants us to know where we belong while we're on earth, to live meaningfully and with a future purpose. He wants us to know where we are going after death and that we need Jesus—now, here, today. This message needs to be spread so all people can live and die peacefully.

SUBMIT

Forgiving the Devil

YOUR QUESTION: Would God forgive the devil if he changed his ways?

SENDER: Daniel, 16

RESPONDER: Brother Paul Terwitte

Of course! I read in the Bible that the devil sinned from the beginning. The Son of God appeared to destroy the works of the devil (1 John 3:8). I recall all the devilish actions that people have performed. But the fact that people will commit these acts is more important to me than the fact that the devils caused them. In the end it is always the human being who is responsible for his actions—good or evil—with or without the devil. In the end, the cross of Christ will outweigh all evil. When all is subjected to the cross, God the Son will subject himself to his Father and God will be in all (1 Cor 15:28).

SUBMIT

Guardian Angels

Do guardian angels exist or are they only inventions of human beings?

SENDER: Simone, 13

RESPONDER: Brother Paul Terwitte

Of course there are guardian angels. They are God's messengers, who tell you that God is protecting you. They can also ask you to do something you might not want to do. They are messengers who come to you very quickly (therefore, they are represented with wings). They are a guarantee to you that God loves you personally and accompanies you. The angels take good care of you and you can depend on them. Whatever happens, they will help you to stay in touch with God. The angels are your protectors on your journey to God. They are also your defenders, who present your good deeds to God. Of course they also know your bad deeds and join you when you ask for God's forgiveness. I firmly believe that I will never be lonely because my angels will accompany me if I drift away from God or good people. My guardian angel will help me find my way back to them again.

SUBMIT

Redemption—
When and From What?

YOUR QUESTION: Did people who lived before the time of Jesus get to heaven? Doesn't the Bible say that he rescued us by his death? From what, our sins? Before Jesus, were the people punished for their sins before they could reach heaven? Today will we go to heaven immediately without going to purgatory?

SENDER: Toby, 22

RESPONDER: Monika Deitenbeck

Galatians 4:4 states: "When the fullness of time had come, God sent his Son, born of a woman, born under the law." And Hebrews 2:14–15 states: "...so that through death he might destroy the one who has the power of death, that is, the devil, and free those who all their lives were held in slavery by the fear of death." Jesus brings life and redemption from death. He saves humans from separation from God and each other. The difficult idea that "the dead are not really dead" developed slowly during Old Testament times. Even in Jesus' day the Sadducees, one of three main Jewish groups, denied life after death. Jesus spoke clearly about resurrection from the dead. We don't know exactly how he saved people who lived before or after him, but he did and will continue to. Jesus took all the evils of humanity with him on the cross, and conquered death. We'll have to wait to find out how he saves us all from death, but we can be certain that his redemptive power holds true for us all.

SUBMIT

Visits after Death

After I die and have been accepted into the kingdom of God, can I look down on people who were dear to me and actually visit them without their knowing it?

SENDER: Simone, 13

RESPONDER: Monika Deitenbeck

Yes and no. This is a tricky question. At the transfiguration, Jesus appeared with Moses and Elijah (Matt 17:1–9) and they talked with one another. This shows that the community of heaven accompanies the community on earth. In the last book of the Bible, Revelation, the praying community in eternity is often described as being before the throne of God. The saints in heaven follow the events on this earth with their prayers. Jesus is the bridge between time and eternity, between those living here on earth and those who "have gone home." We may look forward to a meeting there and we may know that even now our loved ones are with us in some mysterious way. Naturally we should not imagine that they are sitting next to us just to observe us. Do you understand? That is why my initial response to your question was "Yes and no."

SUBMIT

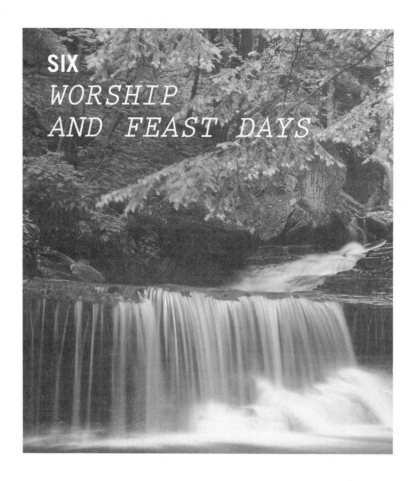

SIX
WORSHIP AND FEAST DAYS

The Last Supper, Vestments, St. Francis,
Corpus Christi, Bells, Good Friday,
Sunday Worship, Incense

Good Friday

YOUR QUESTION: Why does the Catholic pastor lie prostrate on the floor during the Good Friday liturgy?

SENDER: Holly, 15

RESPONDER: Brother Paul Terwitte

On Good Friday, the church is speechless as it celebrates the death of Jesus in the presence of his living body. Through the careful reading of the scripture the presiding priest realizes what happened to Jesus. He thinks of Jesus, who was humiliated by the people of his time as well as by the crucifixion, and all this knowledge makes the participants speechless. Therefore, the ceremony includes the silent entrance of acolytes and priest, the prostration in front of the altar, the lifting of the participants' hands in prayer without greeting one another. There is only one thing they can do—pray. As Jesus went through suffering and death, the priest is praying with us in our needs.

SUBMIT

Celebrating
Feast Days

YOUR QUESTION: Why do we celebrate feasts like Christmas, Corpus Christi, and Easter?

SENDER: Julia, 14

RESPONDER: Marcus C. Leitschuh

People of all times, all cultures, and all religions have celebrated the special events of their time. This is why we joyfully celebrate our birthdays once a year. But then it isn't only we who celebrate our birthday—our parents celebrate with us. We tell stories about our childhood, relate how we were born if there was something unusual about our birth. We recall note-worthy events. We need to celebrate those particular days. At first the Christians celebrated only Easter, because that was the most special event: Jesus is alive, even though he was dead! Later, people became interested in celebrating other events in Jesus' life: his birth, his baptism in the Jordan, his ascension into heaven. The remembrance of these incidents began to be occasions of celebration. Many of these events also became feast days for people of other cultures. Sometimes heathen feasts were changed into Christian feasts, because now people believed in God.

SUBMIT

Sundays in Church

YOUR QUESTION: Why should we go to church on Sundays?

SENDER: Ryan, 13

RESPONDER: Monika Deitenbeck

Serving God has a twofold meaning: God wants to bless us, and we are able to serve God. It is a back-and-forth effort, a mutual meeting, each one making the other happy and showing interest in the other. God wants to give us good things during our path of life, and we give him joy through our presence and openness to him. It is rewarding to go to inspiring services that are good for us and that we like to attend. There are such services. Find them!

SUBMIT

Sundays Again and Again?

YOUR QUESTION: Must we attend church services every Sunday?

SENDER: James, 14

RESPONDER: Marcus C. Leitschuh

In the Catholic Church we have an obligation to attend Sunday services. This stems from the idea that a relationship with God can be true only if it is fostered. If you had a friend whom you visited only a few times a year, he/she would probably want to find someone else who would show interest in him/her more often.

But God too can be visited more often than in church on Sunday. He would like to be with us always. We can talk to him in prayer at any time. Church services, the celebration of Mass and the Eucharist are the highlights in our relationship with God, just as a kiss, a hug, and embracing are high points of contact between persons. But this is not the only time or way that they show their love for one another.

SUBMIT

Women Priests

YOUR QUESTION: Why are there no women priests in the Catholic Church?

SENDER: Maggie, 12

RESPONDER: Brother Paul Terwitte

I am convinced that Jesus gave important roles in the kingdom of God to women as well as to men. The women were very visible in the crowds gathered around Jesus. Women who serve in offices of the church today still have the responsibility of representing Jesus. It is Jesus himself who calls his people together. He gives them the Spirit. He chose men as deacons, priests, and bishops because he himself came from God as a man. He supported women in whatever talents they had as no one else of his time did. However, he chose none of them as apostles.

SUBMIT

Veneration of the Host

Why is the Host venerated in the Catholic Church?

Elizabeth, 22

Brother Paul Terwitte

Jesus gives himself to us personally in the consecrated Hosts. At the Last Supper Jesus said, "This is my Body....Do this in memory of me." Today when the community prays with the priest at the consecration "Lord...let your Spirit come upon these gifts" and the priest says with Jesus, "This is my Body," then Jesus again comes to this earth as he did in Nazareth. I don't just think, "This reminds me of Jesus." No, I trust that Jesus truly comes visibly and personally to be with us until the end of time—in the Host.

SUBMIT

Black versus Colored Vestments

YOUR QUESTION: Why do Evangelical pastors wear black clothing and Catholic clergy wear colored ones?

SENDER: John, 14

RESPONDER: Marcus C. Leitschuh

At the time when Martin Luther wanted to reform the Catholic Church, much money was being lavished on solemn and expensive furnishings of the churches. It did not seem to matter how poor the people who built the churches were. The emphasis was on having beautiful churches in honor of God. With donations toward these church buildings, the people believed they could "buy" a better place in heaven or have their sins forgiven. Martin Luther wanted to return to the essentials of the faith and moved away from expensive pictures and beautiful vestments. For him, the only thing that was to bring color and life was a growth in the understanding of the Bible and the loving grace of God. Today we realize that colored vestments and church decorations are good and are more than an outward exhibition. They can deepen our faith. As in other things in life, too much is bad but in the right measure it is good.

SUBMIT

Noon Bells

YOUR QUESTION: Why do bells in Catholic churches ring at 12:00 noon?

SENDER: Holly, 15

RESPONDER: Brother Paul Terwitte

In 1216 St. Francis of Assisi went on a pilgrimage to a Muslim country and became friends with the Sultan El Melek, which was most unusual during his time. While he was there, St. Francis heard the bells calling the Muslims to prayer. When he returned home he continued to hear the bells ringing in his ears inviting him to prayer. He acted on that experience and asked the church authorities if the bells could ring from the Catholic church towers not only to call the people to Mass services but also to invite them to private prayer, like the Angelus. Since that time the bells in Catholic churches ring three times a day (6:00 a.m., 12:00 noon, and 6:00 p.m.) to invite people to pray the "Angelus" ("The angel of the Lord declared unto Mary...").

SUBMIT

Incense

Why is incense used in Catholic churches?

SENDER: Nelly, 16

RESPONDER: Marcus C. Leitschuh

Incense played an important part in special ceremonies during ancient times. Incense comes from resin, which is burned on glowing coals and forms a fragrant smoke. In ancient times high officials had containers burning with incense carried before them as a sign of honor. The swinging of the incense bowl was later introduced into the Roman court ceremonies. Even later, the practice was carried over into church ceremonies. The custom of swinging the incense before the picture of an emperor was eventually changed to blessing the cross or the Bible in the Christian churches.

SUBMIT

The Lord's Supper

YOUR QUESTION: Why do we celebrate the Lord's Supper and the Eucharist?

SENDER: Dirk, 16

RESPONDER: Marcus C. Leitschuh

The Lord's Supper (Evangelical) and the Eucharist (Catholic) both refer to the last evening meal that Jesus shared with his apostles. There, on the evening before his death, he took bread and wine, said a prayer of thanksgiving and prayed: "This is my body. Do this in memory of me....This chalice is the New Covenant of my blood as often as you drink from it in my memory. As often as you eat of this bread and drink of this blood, you announce the death of the Lord until he comes."

This memorial meal is celebrated in our church services. In it we come very near to God; we can feel him with our hands and can taste him in our mouths. We put ourselves into the place of the apostles at the Last Supper, where they let Jesus serve them and give of himself. Therefore we call it "God's Service" not because we are serving him by our rising early, singing loudly, and paying attention to the homily, but because he serves us.

SUBMIT

SEVEN
ABOUT THE CHURCH

The Faithful, Jews, Confirmation, Luther,
Muslims, Ecumenism, Pope, Relics,
Separated Churches, Celibacy

Totally Obsolete

YOUR QUESTION: I find that the church is totally obsolete. Why do you bind yourselves to beliefs that your Jesus preached two thousand years ago? Isn't that totally out of date?

SENDER: Ed, 15

RESPONDER: Marcus C. Leitschuh

I have a question for you: Is the message that God takes an interest in us and loves us really so old-fashioned? God made human beings. Both he and Jesus were interested in the sick and neglected, especially those who hid in the caves of Gerasa and those who were expelled from society like Matthew. They gave Peter, the weakling, another chance. All that is still true today! If in my free time I take care of people and help them, I do it as a church member who understands how good it is to be a member of the church, as one who wants to live responsibly before God. I keep myself close to God and his ideas concerning other people. God is with me and helps me in a very real way, just as he helps the religious nun who works in a hospital for victims of AIDS in Nigeria, the teacher on Nias Island in Indonesia, and the sister nurse who works for the poor in Bombay.

SUBMIT

Splinter Groups

YOUR QUESTION: Why are there so many different splinter groups among people of Christian faith?

SENDER: Chris, 19

RESPONDER: Monika Deitenbeck

God is complex. There are various types of relationships that we can have with God. People also make different discoveries about God. Depending on their style of worship and the groups in which people feel "at home," they can exercise their faith in one or the other group, wherever they feel that their style of personality is most satisfied.

The Pope

YOUR QUESTION: Is the pope important to my faith?

SENDER: Charlotte, 15

RESPONDER: Marcus C. Leitschuh

More important than the pope is the fact that you are in contact with God. But the Roman Catholic Church sees itself as a worldwide, all-embracing (that is the meaning of "catholic") church. In order to sustain a relationship in all parts around the world, we have the Roman Central Station with the pope as the leader. Rome is the site of this administrative leadership and also the place where bishops meet and great church services are celebrated. In addition to being leader of the church, the pope also serves as vicar of Christ on earth and is also as an ambassador for the church. You can hear his voice even though not everyone likes everything he says.

SUBMIT

Wearing Veils?

Why do nuns wear veils?

SENDER: Sandra, 15

RESPONDER: Brother Paul Terwitte

The nuns want to show everyone that they wish to belong to God alone. It is a tradition that these dedicated women clothe themselves in this particular dress. In time, this practice has changed according to location and culture. But even today there are still men and women who cover themselves, including their heads, to express their decision to be a partner either with another human being or with God. The bridal veil at a wedding has a similar meaning. The woman shows that she will give herself completely to this one partner. A nun wants to give herself completely to God.

SUBMIT

Why a Church?

YOUR QUESTION:
Why do we have a church if it is only a question of faith?

SENDER: Clara, 15

RESPONDER: Monika Deitenbeck

We have a church because our faith in Jesus Christ has a definite influence on our lives. The first Christians always met together, were loyal to one another, celebrated services and feasts, shared joy and pain, and constantly invited others to join them. The Lord of the community sent its members into the world and the community supported them. It is still that way today, but maybe a little more colorful and different from the earliest years of this practice.

SUBMIT

Persecution
of Pagans

YOUR QUESTION: Why were the pagans persecuted, and why did the Christians try very hard to convert them to Christianity in such brutal ways?

SENDER: Scott, no age indicated

RESPONDER: Marcus C. Leitschuh

The persecution of people is one of the cruelest aspects of human history. Christians were persecuted in the first centuries after Christ, Jews during the Nazi era, and so on. Christians persecuted pagans. People have repeatedly used persecution, imprisonment, or killing to solve specific problems. Such force can never be justified, however "worthy" the reason. For example, the Romans thought their government was endangered by Christians who rejected a state religion in which the emperor was considered divine. Sorry to say, religious and political motives were often mixed when Christian rulers wanted to expand their territories. The spread of Christianity was their justification. But conversion may never be by force or violence. "God's offer" is open to all people. Those who reject God or don't want to live in his faith still have human rights on their side: "Thou shalt not kill." Only in self-defense may one threaten or take the life of another. There is no other justification for killing.

SUBMIT

Inactive Pope

YOUR QUESTION: Why didn't the pope do something to prevent the persecution of the Jews and other murders?

SENDER: Paula, 16

RESPONDER: Brother Paul Terwitte

The power of the pope has limits. Even today we experience how difficult it is to end wars. During the Nazi years the pope of that time, Pope Pius XII, personally sheltered three thousand Jews in the *Engelsburg* (Vatican). His diplomats tried to influence the persecutors but did not want to provoke them into placing even more Christians in danger of death. The church tried to influence the Nazis with symbols. That is why the church beatified the simple Capuchin Brother Conrad—as a contrast in character to that of the ruler whom the Nazis elected. The pope really represents the church. Although there were Christians who failed, there were many others who plainly showed that they were on the side of the Jews and other persecuted groups.

SUBMIT

Church

YOUR QUESTION: What is the meaning of "church"?

SENDER: Jerry, 20

RESPONDER: Brother Paul Terwitte

The word *church* comes from the Greek word *ekklesia,* which means "those called together." These are the baptized people. Through baptism, a person belongs to the community of Jesus. The baptized gather around Jesus in the church. They thank God for being called, they listen to his word, they read the Bible, and they talk about it. Then they allow themselves to be strengthened by "participating in the supper." When they then go about their daily work, we hope that they are so enthusiastic about their faith that they take their faith to others through their actions.

Confirmation

YOUR QUESTION: Why should I get confirmed? What do I get from confirmation?

SENDER: Jean, 14

RESPONDER: Monika Deitenbeck

Speaking plainly, those who are being baptized or confirmed receive the necessary instructions to understand the ceremonies. They are given all the information for their introduction into the faith and everything worth knowing about the Lord in whose name they are being baptized or confirmed. At baptism the parents or godparents speak for the child. At confirmation this "yes" to Jesus is that of the person being confirmed. Beyond that we hope our life will become an exciting relationship with the exciting God. We will discover what such a life with God can mean for us.

SUBMIT

Celibacy

YOUR QUESTION: Why do Catholic priests live as celibates? I don't understand why they cannot marry. Didn't God give us the opportunity to continue the human race by having sex? God must have wanted it that way.

RESPONDER: Marcus C. Leitschuh

There is the possibility to continue life through sex, but there is also the possibility to choose a different way of life. It is a free decision, just as some people decide to live a life without marriage, even though they do not become priests or religious men/women. The New Testament speaks of those "who have made themselves eunuchs for the sake of the kingdom of heaven" (Matt 19:12). "For the sake of the kingdom" means that a person wants to keep alive his/her desire for God by remaining unmarried—and without a definite partner something very important is missing from a person's life. A person without a spouse has more energy to serve the community of God, a service that priests and religious perform in a special way. It was not always the rule that priests were not allowed to marry, and the practice differs in the various Christian churches. This rule could undergo further changes with time.

A Different Jesus

YOUR QUESTION: A friend of mine is a Muslim who also knows about Jesus. Is that Jesus different from the Jesus of Christians?

SENDER: Chantal, 14

RESPONDER: Monika Deitenbeck

Yes. In the Islamic faith, Jesus is considered only a human prophet. Christianity is the one religion where God comes to the people. God becomes human in Jesus. Jesus is God in flesh and blood because of God's love for humanity. That is how God redeemed humanity from death—by becoming human, dying for us, and rising again to life. This belief is unique. Only the Christian faith—no other religion—can say that about God.

SUBMIT

Ecumenism

YOUR QUESTION: What does the word *ecumenism* mean?

SENDER: David, 21

RESPONDER: Brother Paul Terwitte

Ecumenism comes from the Greek word *oikoumene* ("inhabited world"). Due to human misunderstandings over the many centuries about what it means to believe in Jesus Christ and how to live as followers, different Christian churches or denominations (e.g., Catholic, Orthodox, Lutheran, Anglican, Baptist, Methodist, Presbyterian, etc.) have come into existence throughout the world. Ecumenism tries to overcome these past historical divisions and to move forward as Christians who seek to work and "live together in the world" as united, rather than divided, in Jesus Christ. Ecumenism attempts to exemplify the prayer of Jesus "that they all may be one" (John 17:21).

SUBMIT

The Greatest Christians

I read that when groups of people are questioned, Mother Teresa of Calcutta, Francis of Assisi, and Martin Luther King are often mentioned as the greatest Christians. What if I cannot do anything as great as they did? How would I begin if I wanted to become famous?

SENDER: Karsten, 18

RESPONDER: Christina Riecke

Do what you can. Leave your usual surroundings. Go to people who live differently from you. Whoever wants to do something unusual must leave his/her usual way of living. Have faith in your views and do not let yourself be deterred from your objective. Talk about what you observe. Engage yourself with others. Listen carefully. Pray for generosity, awareness, and courage.

You might read a few biographies of people who impress you and try to note how they began.

Who, for example, was the inspiration for Martin Luther King's movement? A black seamstress, Rosa Parks, who was supposed to give her place on a bus to a white passenger but remained seated. By doing that she began one of the biggest bus strikes ever. Do what you can. Anyone can remain seated, right?

SUBMIT

Infallibility

YOUR QUESTION: No human being is perfect, but the Pope is infallible. How can that be?

SENDER: Ron, 15

RESPONDER: Marcus C. Leitschuh

Concerning the "infallibility" of the pope, the following was decided by the First Vatican Council in Rome in 1869 and 1870: "When the pope, as first among equal bishops and in community with them, declares a belief to be a dogma of faith, it is binding and free of errors." We say, then, that he is speaking *ex cathedra*, from his chair as teacher. We might say that the pope has the last word in decisions about articles of faith that the church has long believed and that are without contradiction in the Bible.

The only dogma declared by a pope since 1890 is the dogma of the Assumption, the belief that Mary's body was taken up to heaven (1950). All other pronouncements of the pope, including his encyclicals, are to be taken seriously but are not infallible. Pope John Paul II expressed an apology for any mistakes the church may have made in the past.

SUBMIT

Religious Instruction

YOUR QUESTION: Why do we have religion classes?

SENDER: Manuel, 14

RESPONDER: Marcus C. Leitschuh

Religion classes are meant to teach a subject just like classes of math and music. We all live in a culture formed by Christianity. The importance of the Bible and Christianity in the foundation of the modern world should also be learned by those who are not being confirmed during a particular year. Religion teachers do not and may not coerce students to go to church, but they may instruct them. Individual people have to make their own decisions about whether they want to give more attention and time to faith formation. The work of the pastor and co-workers is to begin to create a solid church community.

SUBMIT

Believing

YOUR QUESTION: Why are there still so many people who believe?

SENDER: Stefan, 16

RESPONDER: Monika Deitenbeck

Necessity teaches one to pray. Necessity may also teach one to curse. I know a man who said, "Since I was a soldier during the Second World War I can no longer believe in God." I know another man who said, "If I had not believed in the real existence of God, I could not have made it through the Second World War." These are two different expressions of life, two different ways to handle a similar situation. One man died old and embittered. The other lived to a grand old age and was hopeful and full of confidence in God during his last hour.

SUBMIT

Anointing of the Sick

It was very important for my grandmother that my grandfather receive the last rights before he died. Why do people get the last rights?

SENDER: Jason, 17

RESPONDER: Brother Paul Terwitte

The last rites are sometimes called the anointing of the sick. The Catholic priest is called when someone is very ill. He prays alone or with those who care for sick people, puts his hands on them, and anoints them with the holy oil, which is a special oil consecrated by the bishop. With these actions and as the oil touches the skin, the ill people are made aware of belonging to the community of the church and that God is present. Because this celebration is meant to reconcile the sick person with God and neighbor, it was considered absolutely necessary that a dying person receive this sacrament before death.

SUBMIT

Confirmation

YOUR QUESTION: My Catholic friend has asked for confirmation. She could not explain to me what "confirmation" meant. What is it?

SENDER: Emily, 15

RESPONDER: Brother Paul Terwitte

Baptism, confirmation, and Eucharist are, for a Christian, the introductory sacraments into their faith. The first is baptism, through which one becomes completely connected with Christ. Confirmation says: "Now you are anointed like Jesus: receive the Holy Spirit." The Eucharist says: "Whoever receives this sacrament visibly shows the spiritual life he leads." Through the sacrament of confirmation, the Christian becomes enabled to make Jesus and the community of the church become more visible to the world.

SUBMIT

About the Authors

Monika Deitenbeck-Goseberg (50) is married, has three children, and has been pastor in the Oberrahmede Evangelical Church Community. She is the leader and founder of the Friends of the Homeless in Leidenscheid, leader of the association "God.net," and a member of the committee of the Gerhard Tersteegen Conference.

Marcus Leitschuh (33) is single, a religion teacher in Immenhausen near Kasel. He is well known because of the publication of his several books, among them prayer books for young people. He is a member of the Central Committee of German Catholics.

Christina Riecke (35) is a theologian who works as an evangelist and independent author. She and her husband are active in the community through the "CVJM e/motion" in Essen. She was the main speaker of the Missionary European Project, "The Jesus House."

Brother Paul Terwitte (46) is a Capuchin monk and the superior of the Capuchin Monastery in Frankfurt, Main. He works as a confessor and spiritual director in the inner city Church of Our Lady. Through the Internet he receives many questions from persons who got to know him through his work on television and radio and are looking for answers.